Arthur Johnson Evans

Syracusan Medallions and their Engravers in the Light of Recent

Finds

Arthur Johnson Evans

Syracusan Medallions and their Engravers in the Light of Recent Finds

ISBN/EAN: 9783337250102

Printed in Europe, USA, Canada, Australia, Japan

Cover: Foto ©Andreas Hilbeck / pixelio.de

More available books at **www.hansebooks.com**

SYRACUSAN "MEDALLIONS"

AND THEIR ENGRAVERS
IN THE LIGHT
OF RECENT
FINDS

WITH OBSERVATIONS ON THE CHRONOLOGY AND HISTORICAL
OCCASIONS OF THE SYRACUSAN COIN-TYPES OF THE
FIFTH AND FOURTH CENTURIES B.C.

AND AN ESSAY

ON SOME NEW ARTISTS' SIGNATURES ON
SICILIAN COINS

BY

ARTHUR J. EVANS, M.A., F.S.A.

KEEPER OF THE ASHMOLEAN MUSEUM
AND HON. FELLOW OF BRASENOSE COLLEGE, OXFORD

WITH SEVENTEEN WOODCUTS IN THE TEXT AND TEN AUTOTYPE PLATES

LONDON
BERNARD QUARITCH, 15, PICCADILLY
1892

NOTE.

The first part of this volume, "Syracusan 'Medallions' and their Engravers," is reprinted from the *Numismatic Chronicle* of 1891 (Pt. IV.), with the addition of an Analytical Table of Contents, Index, and two extra plates (VIII. and IX). The paper on "Artists' Signatures on Sicilian Coins" is reprinted, with some slight emendations, from the *Numismatic Chronicle* of 1890

ANALYSIS OF CONTENTS.

SYRACUSAN "MEDALLIONS" AND THEIR ENGRAVERS.

NEW ARTISTS' SIGNATURES ON SICILIAN COINS.

WOODCUTS IN THE TEXT.

SYRACUSAN "MEDALLIONS" AND THEIR ENGRAVERS,

IN THE LIGHT OF RECENT FINDS.

PART I.

INTRODUCTION.

THE "medallions" of Syracuse have been the admiration of the ancient and modern world. From the Seventeenth Century onwards they have been the subject of frequent discussion on the part of numismatic writers, and the historic circumstances connected with the issue of the earliest of them, the *Dâmareteion*, whose name records the wife of Gelôn,[1] arrested the attention of ancient writers, who, as a rule, were little prone to afford us information about numismatic matters.

The view of the earlier numismatists that these fine coins were "medals" in the modern sense of the word, and not intended for circulation, has long been abandoned, and it has been generally recognised that they served, in fact, as current coins, of the value of fifty Sicilian silver *litras*, or ten Attic *drachmæ*. Yet, from their abnormal dimensions, the extraordinary artistic skill devoted to their production and, as will be shown in the course of this

---

[1] For the *Dâmareteion* see Part VI., p. 122 *scqq.*

inquiry, the special circumstances under which they were originally struck, and which place them in a certain degree outside the category of ordinary coins, it does not seem inappropriate, even in the present state of our knowledge, to apply to them the name of " medallions," by which they were till lately generally known. " Medallion," in fact, in the etymological sense of the word, means simply " a large coin," and in this sense Italian numismatists often apply the name " *medaglioncini*," or " small medallions," to tetradrachms, which have nevertheless always been regarded as current coins.

The Syracusan "medallions" struck towards the close of the Fifth Century B.C. have specially arrested attention, on account of the marvellous art that they display.   The heads that appear upon these coins are of two main types —that of the Nymph, Arethusa, with her luxuriant tresses contained in a beaded net ; and an even more beautiful head of the Maiden Goddess, Persephonê,—or, if that name for her should be preferred, Dêmêtêr Chloê,—crowned with the earless barley spray, green and growing, so appropriate to her inner being, as symbolizing the yearly up-springing of Nature to life and light. Of this head Winckelmann remarks that " it transcends all imagining,"[2] and elsewhere he asks : " Might not Raffaelle, who complains that he could not find in Nature any beauty worthy to stand for Galatea, have taken her likeness from the best Syracusan coins, since in his days—with the exception of the Laocoon—the finest statues were not yet discovered ? Beyond these coins human comprehension cannot go."[3]

---

[2] Winckelmann's *Werke* (1808 — 20), iv., **134**. (*Kunstgeschichte* V. c. **2**, § 26.)

[3] Winckelmann (*op. cit.* l. **251**, Erinnerung ueber die Betrachtung der Werke der Kunst). " *Hätte nicht Raphael, dér*

A new interest has, since Winckelmann's time, been
added to these splendid coins by the recognition of the
fact that the names of Kimôn and Evænetos that appear
upon them are those of the artists who engraved the dies,
and who worked for other Sicilian cities besides Syracuse.[4]

---

*sich beklagte zur Galatee keine würdige Schönheit in der Natur
zu finden, die Bildung derselben von der besten Syracusanischen
Münzen nehmen können, da die schönsten Statuen, ausser dem
Laocoon, zu seiner Zeit noch nicht entdecket waren? Weiter als
diese Münzen kann der menschliche Begriff nicht gehen."* Payne
Knight (*Archæologia*, xix. p. 375) says of the Syracusan "medallions," "to the sublime perfection of these coins no work of
man of a similar description has hitherto even approached."

[4] The first to point out that the signature "ΚΙΜΩΝ" represented the name of the engraver was A. von Steinbüchel (in the
Vienna *Jahrbücher der Literatur* (1818), B. II. p. 124; cf. the
Anzeigeblatt for 1833, p. 60). About the same time the same
conclusion was independently put forth by Payne Knight, in his
essay on *The Large Coins of Syracuse* (*Archæologia*, vol. xix.
(1821), p. 369 *seqq.*), who was followed by Noehden, in his
Specimens of Ancient Coins of Magna Græcia and Sicily, from
Lord Northwick's cabinet (London, 1826, p. 41 *seqq.*). Havercamp, in his commentary on Paruta's *Sicilia Numismatica*
(p. 307), had been much puzzled by the name ("Nomen illud
Cimon, seu ΚΙΜΩΝ, me multum torquet," p. 307). He
came to the conclusion that it was a magistrate's name. It is
to the Duc de Luynes (*Annali dell' Instituto*, &c., 1830, p. 85),
and Raoul Rochette, in his *Lettre à M. le Duc de Luynes sur les
Graveurs des Monnaies Grecques* (Paris, 1831, p. 19 *seqq.*),
that the credit belongs of first detecting in the signature
"EYAINE" beneath the head of Persephonê on the fellow-
medallions, the name of the engraver, Evænetos (EYAINE-
TOϹ), which occurs in a fuller form on tetradrachms of
Syracuse and Katanê. These conclusions as to the true
meaning of the signature on these coins have been borne out
by more recent writers: [cf., especially Von Sallet, *Die Künst-
lerinschriften auf griechischen Münzen* (Berlin, 1871); Head,
Coins of Syracuse (1874), p. 19 *seqq.*; Poole, *Brit. Mus.
Cat.,—Sicily*; Gardner, *Types of Greek Coins*, and the excellent
work of Dr. Rudolf Weil, *Die Künstlerinschriften der sicilischen
Münzen* (Berlin, 1884, p. 10 *seqq.*; 19, &c.)]. Brunn,
(*Künstlergeschichte*, ii. 248) almost alone amongst modern writers,

Various efforts have been made in this connexion to
contrast the style of these two artists, but the scale has
generally weighed in Evænetos's favour. "If we only
possessed Kimôn's piece," observes Lenormant, "it would
justly awaken in us our entire admiration and would be
cited as a type of inimitable perfection. But it pales
beside the work of Evænetos. The style of Kimôn—
superior as it still is to the finest works that the Renais-
sance itself has produced in monetary art—appears smaller
by comparison with the other. . . . Kimôn is a great artist:
Evænetos is the greatest of all in the branch that he has
cultivated. He is the Pheidias of coin-engraving."[5] As

---

refuses to allow that the signature on Evænetos' dekadrachms
and gold pieces refers to the engraver, although he accepts
the view that the smaller signature with this name on the
tetradrachms is an engraver's signature. So, too, at Katanê,
he allows that the signature EYAINETO on the tetradrachms is an artist's signature; but the EYAI which
appears more conspicuously on drachms of the same style,
with the head of Amenanos, cannot, he says, be accepted as
such. "Otherwise," he continues, "we lose every criterion for
distinguishing an engraver's name from any other." According
to this view, then, it is more reasonable to believe that there
were two contemporaries named Evænetos at Syracuse, both
signing on the coins, one a die-sinker and the other not, and
that the same extraordinary coincidence occurred at Katanê!
But, as I have pointed out in my *Horsemen of Tarentum*
(p. 116 *seqq.*), the coin-engravers of Sicily and Great Greece
sign in two qualities, both as artists and as responsible mint
officials. Sometimes one character is conspicuous in the signature and sometimes the other (cf., too, Weil, *op. cit.* p. 24).
For Kinch's theory, see p. 136.

   [5] *Gazette des Beaux-Arts*, 1863 (15), p. 338, 339. Mr. Head
in his *Historia Numorum* (p. 155), says, "Of these two
magnificent dekadrachms (of Kimôn and Evænetos), one that is
signed by Euainetos is the *chef d'œuvre* of the art of coin-
engraving." Mr. Poole, *Greek Coins as Illustrating Greek Art*
(*Num. Chron.*, 1864, p. 244, *seqq.*), also gives the palm to
Evænetos. He admits that "nothing more delicately finished

to the actual school to which the works of Kimôn and
Evænetos are to be referred, Lenormant would detect that
of Polykleitos rather than Pheidias; but there seems, in
truth, to be no good reason for seeking the artistic traditions here represented beyond the three seas of Sicily.[6]

Certainly we have not here the bold and simple style
of some of the coins of Greece proper, and the detail and
ornament of these "medallions" has been a stumbling-
block to some who would transfer the canons of high art
in sculpture to the narrow field on which the die-sinker
exercised his craft. But it was precisely because the
great Sicilian engravers took a juster view of the require-
ments of their special branch of art that they attained, at
such a surprisingly early date,[7] a perfection not to be
found elsewhere in Hellas, and that their masterpieces
surpassed in beauty and interest all but a very few exceptional pieces to be found throughout the length and
breadth of the Greek world. The gem-like finish of the
details, the decorative richness, the more human beauty
of the features that they represented, the naturalistic
gleanings from the Sicilian fields around—from air and

---

has been produced by Greek art " than Evænetos' Persephonê,
and that " the first impression is very pleasing," but complains
that, " you cannot magnify it without becoming aware of a
want of expression," and that the treatment of the hair is
intensely artificial, with shell-like and snake-like curls that are
suggestive of the hot irons and 'artists in hair' of conventional
life." Lenormant, on the other hand, remarks, " Regardez
pendant quelque temps une monnaie gravée par Evénète et
bientôt vous oublierez les dimensions exiguës de l'objet que
vous tenez à la main."

[6] Some terra-cotta female heads from Syracuse and the
neighbourhood show much the same artificial arrangement of
the locks of hair as is seen beneath the net on Kimôn's "medallions" (cf. Kekulé, *Die Terracotten von Sicilien*, Taf. x.).

[7] Cf. Gardner, *Types of Greek Coins*, p. 131.

sea—thrown into their designs, were regarded by the artists of these dies as altogether appropriate to this class of small relief in metal-work.

It is by this standard of appropriateness, and by no other, that the masterpieces of Kimôn and Evænetos, and that of another Artist, of whose work we shall presently speak, must be judged. To the greater works of Greek statuary and relief, in ivory or marble, warmth and variety, and even minute detail, far beyond our present ken, was supplied by calling in the painter's and the goldsmith's art. Even in bronze-work monotony was avoided by the inlaying and overlaying with gold and silver; diamonds might sparkle in the eyes, diadems and torques of precious metal might glitter about head and neck, and the helm or shield of God or Hero might glow with many-hued enamels. But in the smooth, glistening surface of a coin there was no opportunity for such adventitious adornments—polychrome, chryselephantine, or the like. Limited in relief, the outlines yet could not be thrown up by colour contrasts. Hence, according to the canons of Greek taste, there was the greater need for luxuriant detail and minutely decorative treatment of surfaces; for the avoidance of bare backgrounds[8] by a more picturesque treatment of the design itself, and the insertion of accessory objects of beauty; for

---

[8] In the case of too many coins of Greece proper this is effected by the procrustean process of cutting their background off altogether and covering almost the whole field with the central design. Nothing, for instance, can be nobler than some heads of Zeus and Hèra on the coins of Elis. But they are designed for dies half as large again as those actually used. They remind us of gems torn from their sockets. There is a clipped air about such coins.

infusing the divine forms portrayed with a greater glow
of liveliness and life to make up for the golden hair, the
flashing eyes and roseate lips, that were beyond the reach
of the die-sinker's art, but which, in the case of the
greater works of sculpture, might serve to reconcile
severer outlines. It was this which the Sicilian engravers
instinctively perceived, and it is this which raises them,
in their own profession, above the level of their fellow-
workers in the greater art centres of the Mother-Country,
who seem too often to have misconceived the true conditions of their craft.

Of what this art of the Sicilian coin-engravers was
capable at its best, a new and splendid illustration has
been now supplied by a recent find brought to light on
the slopes, and from beneath the lava, of Mount Etna.
The piece in question, which is a principal theme of the
present monograph, and which will be of interest not
to numismatists only but to all lovers of art in its widest
sense, is nothing less than a Syracusan "medallion" by
a New Artist. His designs, as shown by this coin, may be
set beside the works of the two rival engravers without
losing by the comparison, while, in some respects, they
strike a higher note than either. The head of Korê,
indeed, that he has here created for us, is a vision of beauty,
transcending any impersonation of the Maiden Goddess
that has been handed down to us from ancient times. It
has, moreover, a special value from the light it throws on
the same portrait on the dekadrachms of Evænetos, and
as supplying a new and unhoped-for standpoint of comparison for surveying the masterpiece of that engraver.
And, as will be shown in detail in the course of this study,[9]

---

[9] See p. 39 *seqq.*

there are grounds for believing that the head of Persephonê, as she appears on his famous "medallions," is,
in its main outlines, derived from that of the New Artist,
though the more modern genius of Evænetos has assimilated and transformed it.

The hoard which contained this unique monument of
medallic art has also supplied a new and later version of
the "medallion" types of Evænetos, presenting, for the first
time, his signature in full.   The deposit itself, of which
a summary account will be given in the succeeding section,
was chiefly composed of Syracusan "medallions," by Kimón
and Evænetos, and this hoard, together with a further
important find of Greek and Siculo-Punic coins, recently
unearthed in Western Sicily,[10] has supplied some new and
valuable data for determining the chronology of these
splendid pieces, and for enabling us to solve more than
one problem connected with the Syracusan coin types of
the last quarter of the Fifth, and the first of the Fourth,
Century B.C.

For, great as has been the interest attaching to these
"medallions," many of the most elementary questions regarding them remain unsolved. Earlier writers, who judged
a Greek type as they would a Roman, had no difficulty in
tracing on the panoply on the reverse of these coins a
direct reference to a victory in war gained by the Syracusans, though they might differ as to what triumph it commemorated.[11] In more recent times the better view has pre-

---

[10] See Appendix A.

[11] So, for example, Don Vincenzo Mirabella, in his *Dichiara-
zioni della Pianta dell' antice Siracuse e d'alcune scelte Medaglie
d'esse* (Naples, 1613, *Medaglie*, p. 29), writes of one of Kimón's
"medallions": "*l'arme ... poste di sotto, significano quelle de
gl'inimici vinti, escludono i pensieri di coloro che han creduto*

vailed that the trophies seen beneath the chariot on the
reverse of these coins, coupled, as they are, with the inscription AΘΛΑ, must, primarily at least, be referred to
an agonistic contest.[12] With regard to the date of these
"medallion" issues, again, various views have been put
forward, on the grounds of style and epigraphy. The
Duc de Luynes attributed them to the last years of
Dionysios the Elder, or to the reign of the younger
tyrant of the same name.[13] Von Sallet brings down
even the earlier work of the Syracusan artist, Phrygillos, to the Fourth Century, "several decennia before
Philip of Macedon."[14] Leake considered that the occur-

---

*essere stata intagliata per vittoria sacra ò di Giouochi Olimpici, ò
somiglianti. Restarebbe a vedere; se per qualche congettura potes-
simo intendere, per qual particolar vittoria fosse ella stata ordi-
nata, se contra gli Ateniesi, Cartaginesi ò Siciliani, il che certo
sarebbe temerità, voler di certo affermare."* In spite of this
caution, he inclines, on account of the great size of the coins,
to the victory over the Athenians. Havercamp, in his com-
mentaries on Paruta's *Sicilia Numismatica* (Leyden, 1723, p.
306), connects these coins with Timoleôn's triumph over the
Carthaginians.

[12] Eckhel's position (*Doctrina Numorum*, i. 243) is somewhat intermediate. "Quoniam numi praesentes eximii sunt
voluminis ac ponderis verisimile est factum aliquo tempore ut
qui virtute panopliam essent promeriti numis his publice dona-
rentur. Erant qui malent haec praemia ad relatas in ludis vic-
torias referre. At tum horum erit commemorare etiam exempla
victores in ludis panoplia donari fuisse solitos." Noehden,
Specimens of Ancient Coins of Magna Graecia and Sicily, p. 42,
seqq., rightly meets this objection.

[13] *Numismatique des Satrapies* (1846), p. 63. This must be
considered a rectification of his earlier view (*Revue Numismatique*, 1840, p. 24), that they belonged to Hiketas' time—a
conclusion based on the fact that Evaenetos' head of Persephonê
was imitated on Hiketas' gold coinage.

[14] *Künstlerinschriften auf Griechischen Münzen* (1871), p. 40.
"*Die Zeit welcher die Silber- und Kupfermünzen des Phrygillos
angehören wird durch das kurze O im Stadtnamen, durch die*

rence of the Ω on the dekadrachms showed that they were later than 403;[15] on the other hand, from the signature EYAINETO, on the earlier tetradrachms by Evænetos, he places these in the Fifth Century. His conclusion with regard to the dekadrachms of both artists is, that they belong to the time of Dionysios I. It had been already urged by Payne Knight[16] that it was "to the combination of power, skill, wealth, liberality, and ambition," represented by the Dionysii, that these "medallions" were owing; and this view, which has, as we have seen, met with general favour by numismatists, has derived powerful support from Mr. Head's careful classification of the Syracusan coin-types in his special work on that subject[17] and, again, more recently, in his *Historia Numorum*.[18]

The result of the present inquiry is, in one direction, to confirm the prevalent view so far as it concerns the reign of Dionysios I., but in another direction to go beyond it, and to show that the earliest issues of these "medallions" must be referred to the moment of exultation and expansion that immediately followed the Athenian overthrow. This conclusion is based not only on the evidence brought to light by the recent discoveries but on extensive typo-

---

auch bei *Eumenos* vorkommende *Rückseite* mit EYΘ, *und durch die Bustrophedon-Legende des Namens ungefähr bestimmt; man kann die Münzen in das vierte Jahrhundert, mehrere Decennien vor Philipp von Macedonien setzen.*" Friedländer, *Arch. Zeit.* 31 (1874), p. 102, places the coinage of these dekadrachms in the Fourth Century.

[15] *Transactions of the Royal Society of Literature* (2nd series, 1850, p. 361), and cf. *Numismata Hellenica*, p. 73.

[16] *Archæologia*, xix. (1821) p. 374.

[17] *Coins of Syracuse*, pp. 20, 21. Dr. Weil (*Künstlerinschriften*, &c., p. 30) takes a similar view, carrying back the earliest of these dekadrachms to the end of the Fifth Century.

[18] P. 154.

logical studies, and, in a principal degree, on data supplied
by the more or less contemporary coinages of Western
Sicily—Greek, Punic, and Elymian. The "medallions" of
Evænetos and the commoner of Kimôn's issues may be
safely brought within the limits of the Dionysian period.
But some earlier specimens of Kimôn's handiwork, the
chronological importance of which has been curiously overlooked, perhaps too the noble piece by the New Artist, can
be shown to go back to a somewhat earlier date. Moreover,
the approximate year to which, by a variety of concordant
indications, this first re-issue of *pentêkontalitra* of the old
Dâmareteian standard can be traced back corresponds so
exactly with the date of the great victory over the Athenians that we are able, as in the case of the prototype
struck after Gelôn's defeat of the Carthaginians, to establish an occasion at once religious and historical for this
numismatic revival. In other words, the first issue of
these later "medallions," with the prize trophy beneath
the racing chariot, connects itself in the most natural way
with the New Games instituted at Syracuse to commemorate the "crowning mercy" of the Assinaros.

Apart, however, from this numismatic record of one of
the most tragic episodes in history, which this inquiry
seems to establish, the fresh chronological data brought
out by this comparative study lead to some new conclusions regarding the dates of the Syracusan coin-types in
general, belonging to the best period of art.

These conclusions, to which attention has already been
partly directed in my paper "On some New Artists' Signatures,"[19] tend to throw back what may be called the Period
of the Signed Coinage at Syracuse to an earlier date than

---

[19] *Num. Chron.*, 1890, p. 296 *seqq.* (p. 173 *seqq.* of the present
volume).

had hitherto been thought possible. On the other hand, they expose a lacuna in the tetradrachm coinage during the Dionysian period which suggests some curious numismatic problems.

The result to which we are inevitably led by these typological researches is, that by about 400 B.C., the tetradrachm issues of Syracuse entirely break off. The noble *pentêkontalitra*, from the early days of Dionysios' tyranny onwards struck abundantly by the Syracusan mint, stand forth as the sole representatives of the large silver issue during this period, as if any smaller denomination were unworthy of Syracusan magnificence. What tetradrachms there were in circulation, excepting the survivals from the abundant issues of earlier date, were supplied by the "camp-coinage" of the Carthaginian mercenaries and the autonomous pieces of the half-independent Punic cities of the Island. The small change was, however, to a far larger degree provided by the " Pegasi " or ten-litra staters of the Mother-City, Corinth, and some sister colonies, till such time as the Syracusans began to strike them in their own name. This first coinage of Syracusan " Pegasi " dates, as will be shown by a conclusive example, from the time of Diôn's expedition.

PART II.

ON A HOARD CHIEFLY CONSISTING OF SYRACUSAN DEKADRACHMS, FOUND AT SANTA MARIA DI LICODIA, SICILY.

In January of last year a peasant digging in his plot of land at Santa Maria di Licodia, a small town that lies on one of the Westernmost spurs of Etna, found a pot containing over eighty silver coins, no less than sixty-seven of which were Syracusan dekadrachms or *pentêkontalitra*. According to the account given me, the deposit lay beneath a layer of lava. The coins were at once taken into Catania, where I saw them a few days afterwards, and was thus fortunate enough not only to be able to take down a summary record of the contents of this remarkable hoard, but to secure at least temporary possession of some of the most interesting specimens. A portion of the coins, perhaps owing to the action of the lava, had suffered considerably, large parts of the surface having flaked off on one or other of their faces. There were, however, among them about a score of "medallions" in really brilliant condition, including one which from the unique type presented both by its obverse and reverse, and from the marvellous beauty and finish of its design, must take its place among the greatest masterpieces of Syracusan art that have come down to our time. The following is a brief account of the hoard.

SYRACUSE.

Dekadrachms by Kimôn.

1. *Obv.*—Head of Arethusa, in net, in low relief (Type
   I.). **Inscr.** ΣYPAKOΣIΩN. KI / M on
   band of the sphendoné above the forehead.

   Rev.—Quadriga, &c., in Kimôn's usual style, and
   KIMΩN on exergual line of reverse. (Pl.
   I., fig. 5. As *B.M. Cat., Syracuse,* No. 100.)   2

   [In good condition.]

2. *Obv.*—Head of Arethusa, in net, in different style
   and high relief. (Type II., var.) KI on band.
   (It is uncertain whether an inscription also
   existed on the dolphin beneath the head.)

   Rev.—As before. Inscription, AΘΛΛ, visible beneath panoply 1

   [Somewhat worn; **obverse** die shows traces of
   fracture.]

3. *Obv.*—Similar head to No. 2. (Type II., var.) Inscription, K on band, which is exceptionally
   broad. No inscription on dolphin.

   Rev.—Same. (Cf. Pl. II., fig. 1; *B. M. Cat.* 205, 206.)   2

   [Head in **one case** well preserved, in the other fair.
   The reverses of both much worn.]

4. *Obv.*—Head as No. 3 but in finer style. (Type III.,
   A.) K on band, which is narrower; KIMΩN
   on dolphin.

   Rev.—As before 2

   [Well **preserved.** Of one of **these coins** I saw only
   the obverse, the original reverse was probably in bad condition and it had been
   accordingly sliced **off** and replaced by a
   reverse of a **medallion** by Evænetos, **the**
   head of which had been probably defective.
   This ingenious fraud, which came under my
   notice some time after the date **of** the dis-

covery of the hoard, was so well executed
that it had already deceived one practised
numismatist. It was no doubt executed by
the notorious Catanian coin-forger, Bianchi.)

5. *Obv.*—Head of similar type to No. 4, but of coarser
    workmanship. (Type III., B.) **K** on band
    and **KIMΩN** on dolphin beneath neck.

   Rev.—Similar. (*B. M. Cat.* 202, 203). . . 1

   [Obverse well preserved and freshly struck. The
   reverse, however, seems to have been struck
   from a die that had become much oxidized.]

Dekadrachms by Evænetos.

6. *Obv.*—Head of Persephonê to l., wreathed with
    barley leaves. Inscr., **ΣYPAKOΣIΩN**
    above; around, **four** dolphins; and beneath
    the head full signature, **EYAINETOY**.

   Rev.—Quadriga, with horses in high action. Nikê
   above and panoply below (Pl. V., fig. 14; Cf.
   B. M. Cat., Syracuse, 175, &c.) . . . 1
   [In brilliant preservation.]

7. *Obv.*—Head of Persephonê wreathed with barley
    leaves as before. Signature **EYAINE**
    more or less visible beneath the head.

   Rev.—Quadriga, with horses in high action, and
   arms below. In one instance the inscription
   AΘΛΑ was visible below. (Pl. V., fig. 13;
   B. M. Cat. 175.) 15

   [In various states of preservation. Some brilliant.
   The reverses especially had in some cases
   much suffered from sulphurous action; in
   other instances the reverse die showed signs
   of wear and oxidization.]

8. *Obv.*—Similar, but **Δ** beneath chin; **EYAINE**, as
    before, beneath head.

   Rev.—Similar. (Pl. V., fig. 12; *B. M. Cat.* No. 173.) 4

   [Fair preservation, but in one case the reverse die
   had been in a foul (probably oxidized) condition when the coin was struck.]

No. of coins
in hoard.

9. *Obv.*—Similar, but no signature or letter in f. visible.[1]

   Rev.—Similar 15

   [Various states of preservation. The reverses especially had in several instances much suffered from sulphurous action.]

10. *Obv.*—Similar head, &c. No signature or letter in f. Globule under chin.

   Rev.—Similar. (*B. M. Cat.* 179.) . . . 7

   [Mostly badly preserved.]

11. *Obv.*—Similar head, &c. No signature or letter in f. Dot or globule beneath chin, and behind head, cockleshell.

   Rev.—Similar 1

   [Fair, but reverse die had been considerably worn before the coin was struck.] .

12. *Obv.*—Similar head, &c. No dot beneath chin, but cockleshell behind head.

   Rev.—Similar. (Pl. V. 11; *B. M. Cat.* 186.) . 13

   [Various states of preservation, from fine to indifferent.]

13. *Obv.*—Similar head; no dot; behind head a star of eight rays.

   Rev.—Similar. (*B. M. Cat.* 185.) . . . 1

   [Somewhat worn.]

14. *Obv.*—Similar head. Behind, to r., a head of a griffin.

   Rev.—Similar. (*B. M. Cat.* 187.) . . . 1

   [Indifferently preserved.]

Dekadrachm by a New Artist.

15. *Obv.*—Head of Persephonè in a severer style, and with more flowing hair. Inscription: ΣΥΡΑΚΟΣΙΩΝ, removed to lower circumference of coin.

---

[1] It is, however, probable that had these coins been better struck the signature ΕΥΑΙΝΕ would have been found.

No. of coins
in hoard.

Rev.—Quadriga, &c., in new style, passing stand (?); action of horses less high and more rhythmic; arms larger and more ornate; and inscription, **AΘΛΛ**, in large letters above shield. In r. hand corner of exergue, signature **NK** or **HK** (?) in microscopic characters. Pl. IV., and p. 30, fig. 1. (For full description, v. *infra*, p. 27 *seqq*.) 1

[Brilliant condition.]

Syracusan Tetradrachms.

16. *Obv.*—Dàmaretēion type. (*B. M. Cat.* 64.) . . 1

[Worn.]

17. *Obv.*—Style of Eumenés . . . 2

[Somewhat worn.]

18. *Obv.*—**ξYPAKOξIOξ**. By Eukleidas (?) (As *B. M. Cat.* 192.)

Rev.—As *B. M. Cat.* 194, &c. 1

[Well preserved.]

19. *Obv.*—[**ξYPAKOξIΩN**]. Female head to r. in *korymbos*. (*B. M. Cat.* 180.) (Cf. p. 146, fig. 10). *Rev.*—Persephonè, &c. (*B. M. Cat.* 224.) . . 1

[In bad condition.]

20. *Obv.*—[**ξYP** . . . .] By Phrygillos: traces of insc. **ΦPY** on band of *sphendonê*. (See *Num. Chron.* 1890, Pl. XVIII, 6*b*. Cf. *B M. Cat.* 158.)

Rev.—Probably by Evarchidas (v. *infra*, p. 131). Persephonè holding torch, crowned by Nikê, who also holds aplustre. (Cf. *B. M. Cat.* 224.) 1

[A good deal oxidized, otherwise fair.]

MESSANA. *Tetradrachms.*

21. Transitional type: olive-leaf beneath biga (*B. M. Cat.* 26.) 1

[Worn.]

No. of coins
in hoard.

22. Somewhat later Transitional type; dolphin under
hare; two dolphins beneath biga.. (Cf.
B. M. Cat. 38.) 1

[Worn.]

23. *Obv.*—ΜΕϹϹΑΝΙΟΝ. Head of Pelorias, beneath
hare, with inscription, ΠΕΛΩΡΙΑϹ, round
it.

Rev.—Biga of mules galloping. (See Pl. X. 3*a*,
and p. 186 *seqq.*, for full description, &c.) 1

[Somewhat worn.]

SELINÛS. *Tetradrachm.*

24. *Obv.*—As *B. M. Cat.* 30.

Rev.—Apollo and Artemis in slow quadriga, behind
which is an ear of barley 1

[Fair condition.]

MOTYA. *Tetradrachm.*

25. *Obv.*—Head copied from the Arethusa on Kimôn's
dekadrachm. Type II.

Rev.—Crab. (Cf. Pl. II., 8.) . . . 1

[Slightly worn.]

26. ATHENS. *Tetradrachms.* Archaic Style . . 2

SUMMARY OF HOARD.

SYRACUSE :

Dekadrachms by Kimôn		8
Dekadrachms by Evænetos, signed 20 ⎫		58
unsigned 38 ⎭		
Dekadrachm by New **Artist** . . .		1
Tetradrachms		6
MESSANA, Tetradrachms		3
SELINÛS, Tetradrachm		1
MOTYA, Tetradrachm		1
ATHENS, Tetradrachms		2

Total 80

There were, in addition to the above, a certain number of " Pegasi," but these had unfortunately been mixed up by the owner with a quantity of similar coins from another source.

It may be convenient first to consider the few non-Syracusan coins discovered in this remarkable deposit. Of these the tetradrachm of Motya, the obverse of which represents a copy by a Siculo-Punic artist of the profile head of Arethusa in the net, as seen on Kimôn's deka-drachms, is of the greatest rarity. The Selinuntine reverse type, on which a large barley spike shoots up behind the chariot, appears to be a new variety.[2] The most important among the non-Syracusan coins found in the Santa Maria hoard is unquestionably the Messanian tetradrachm already published in the *Numismatic Chronicle*.[3]

Of the Syracusan tetradrachms contained in the hoard, the most remarkable was that with an obverse signed by the artist Phrygillos, associated with a reverse type by the newly discovered engraver Evarchidas, about which enough has also been said in the above-cited paper.

It is, however, with the Syracusan dekadrachms constituting the great bulk—sixty-seven out of eighty—of the Santa Maria deposit, that we are on the present occasion specially concerned. Of these, eight were the work of Kimôn, fifty-eight of Evænetos, and one of a hitherto unknown artist.

In the case of both of the two former engravers, the hoard supplies internal evidence that the issue of these silver fifty-litra pieces must at the time of their deposit

---

[2] This coin has since been acquired for the Museum of Palermo.

[3] Vol. x. 3rd Ser. (1890), p. 285 *seqq. New Artists' Signatures on Sicilian Coins* (p. 186 *seqq.* of the present volume).

have been already many years in duration. Not only do we find a considerable variety of types, but the signs of wear displayed by many of the coins show that they had been already several years in circulation. Other examples again afford interesting evidence that the dies themselves had in some cases suffered considerable damage in the course of use. Thus the obverse die of No. 2, signed by Kimón, had sustained a fracture, and, on the other hand, the reverse dies of several dekadrachms of Evænetos and one of Kimón were evidently in a very foul condition at the time that the coins were struck, the impressions showing evident traces of the oxidization of the matrices.[4] The reverse dies in other cases had been much worn.[5]

The dekadrachms signed by Kimón, which—for reasons to be fully stated later on—I have placed first in my list, afford interesting evidence of artistic evolution. The earliest of his Arethusa heads, No. 1, is executed in the flat relief of the preceding Syracusan coinage, and stands, as we shall see, in an intimate relation to an early tetradrachm type of Evænetos. To this succeeds the effigy in bold relief, of which, however, there is traceable an earlier and a later class. Of the earlier class, No. 3 is a good example; it approaches the flatter original head in the broad character of the sphendonê band above the forehead. Finally, on the third class exemplified by the obverse of 4 and 5 the band is narrower. These classes have been distinguished in my list as Types I., II., and III.

The dekadrachms of Evænetos found in this deposit consist of nine main types,[6] and as in the case of Kimón's

---

[4] Cf. especially Nos. 5, 7, and 8.
[5] Cf. Nos. 7, 11.
[6] Owing to the somewhat summary study of the bulk of these coins, to which, by the circumstances of the case, I was

coinages, show greater variety in the obverse than in the
reverse designs. The types represented in the find are
already known, with one remarkable exception, but some
of the specimens are of interest from their brilliant condition and the illustration that they supply of variations
on points of detail. The reverse of a specimen of No. 12
(Pl. V. fig. 10) exhibits a very beautiful figure of Nikê, with
a waving top-knot on her head, a feature not yet noticed
on these coins. It is remarkable that in only a single case,
the very beautiful coin reproduced on Pl. V. fig. 12, and
Pl. IX., was the legend AΘΛΛ beneath the arms in the
exergue clearly defined. The obverse head of this piece,
beneath which the upper part of the signature EYAINE is
visible, is also of extraordinary merit, and with the fine
coin with Δ in the field reproduced in Pl. V. fig. 11, gives
a good idea of the masterpieces of this artist at his best.

From a comparison of the style of the different types
represented, it results that some of the unsigned dekadrachms are slightly anterior in date to the earliest of
those on which the signature of Evænetos appears. These
early characteristics are especially noteworthy on the coins
with a cockle behind the head of Korê (Pl. IV., fig. 10),
which are conspicuous for their larger and grander rendering of the Goddess's head, as well as for the less
sensational character of the chariot group on the reverse.
Of the signed dekadrachms, the earliest seem to be those
reading " EYAINE," accompanied by the letter Δ in the
field, which in all probability must be regarded as an
indication of value, and as standing for Δεκάξραχμον.

---

obliged to restrict myself, I have not in the case of Evænetos'
coins attempted to indicate all the varieties of die or of detail in
the arrangement of the civic inscription.

Of all the types of Evænetos represented in this hoard, the latest is unquestionably No. 6, on which the signature appears at full length as **EYAINETOY**.[7] This interesting type seems to be altogether unpublished. No coin with this inscription or of this type exists either in the National Collection or in any to which I have had access. A single example of this type occurred in the present hoard, and a phototype of it is given on Pl. V. fig. 14. It will be seen that the head of Korê on this coin is remarkably small and lacks the grandeur of some of Evænetos' earlier works. The hair is less wavy and luxuriant. The quadriga shows very high action and belongs to the more sensational reverse types of this artist. The weight of this dekadrachm is 663 grains (42·9 grammes).

The most remarkable discovery brought to light by the present hoard is, however, unquestionably the dekadrachm summarily described under No. 15. It represents the work of a new and hitherto unknown artist on the Syracusan dies, and though the head of Korê that it exhibits shows distinct affinities to the type of Evænetos, both the obverse and reverse of this truly magnificent piece present specialities of style, design, and epigraphy which place it in a category by itself.

Leaving this coin to be fully described and discussed in the following section, and taking a retrospective survey of the hoard as a whole, we may obtain a few indications

---

[7] In *Historia Numorum*, p. 154, the full inscription EYAI-NETOY is cited as accompanying the coin referred to as Fig. 100, which is taken from a specimen in the British Museum (*Cat.* No. 178) and in which the Δ appears in the field of the obverse. Mr. Head, however, informs me that this is due to a printer's error, and that the last three letters of the signature should have been in brackets. The full legend EYAINETOY, as seen on the Santa Maria piece is associated with a much later head. This coin is now in Mr. H. Montagu's cabinet.

bearing on the date of its deposit. The general character of tetradrachm types associated with the "medallions," is unquestionably somewhat earlier than we should have otherwise expected. Yet it must be observed that the same peculiarity was present in an even more marked degree in the important find of coins recently made in Western Sicily, described by Professor Salinas, in which dekadrachms, both of Kimôn and Evænetos, were associated with Sicilian tetradrachm types, the great bulk of which belonged to the period when O was still in use in place of Ω.

Of the present find the coin of Selinûs showed the older epigraphy, as did two of the Messanian tetradrachms, while the third of that city illustrated the transition from O to Ω, the older form being adhered to in the civic name, the new appearing in the name of the Nymph Pelôrias. Of the Syracusan tetradrachms, one belonged to the older Dâmareteian type, two were the work of Eumenês, one, No. 18, probably by Eukleidas, who uses the form ϹYPAKOϹIOϹ, which skilfully avoids the necessity of pronouncing between the older and the newer letter-form, and may be regarded as a characteristic product of the time of transition. The obverse of the coin signed by Phrygillos (No. 20), unfortunately does not show the termination of the civic inscription, but this artist employs both forms of orthography. No. 19 alone, though very badly preserved, unquestionably originally bore the inscription ϹYPAKOϹIΩN.

It would, I think, be unsafe to bring down any of these types beyond 405 B.C., while most of them are certainly anterior to 410. On the other hand, from the fact that on the dekadrachms the use of the newer form of Ω is universal, and that at the time when this hoard was deposited many of them had evidently been several years in circulation, it is probable that the more recent, at least, belong to a distinctly later date than any of the tetradrachms with which they were associated.

Santa Maria di Licodia, where the present hoard was discovered, corresponds, approximately at least, with the site of the Sikel stronghold of Inêssa that lay between Hadranum and the Galeatic Hybla, on the ledge of lower hills immediately below Mount Etna to the South-West.[8] On the removal hither of the population of Hierôn's Ætna from Katanê, in 461, this city succeeded to the name of Ætna, by which it was henceforth known. The successful operations of the Carthaginians during the first years of the Fourth Century B.C. against Messana and Katanê, induced Dionysios to withdraw to this place the Campanian mercenaries, hitherto stationed, in the Syracusan interest,[9] at the latter city, and henceforth, to Timoleôn's time, Ætna became a stronghold of the Dionysian dynasty.

Considering that the site of the present discovery lies in the neighbourhood of Katanê, with which Ætna-Inêssa was historically so intimately connected, the entire absence of Katanæan coins from this hoard itself affords strong evidence that it was withdrawn from circulation at a period when the autonomous coinage of Katanê itself had for some time ceased, while, on the other hand, the fact that seventy-three out of eighty coins were from Syracusan dies points strongly to the conclu-

---

[8] *Strabo*, vi., 2, 8, and 23. Freeman, *Sicily*, vol. i. p. **148**.

[9] *Diodôros*, lib. xiv. c. 60. The Campanian mercenaries seem to have withdrawn to Ætna between the capture of Messana by Himilkôn in 396 B.C., and the capture of Katanê which resulted on the naval victory of Magôn. For a moment Ætna became the headquarters of Dionysios himself.

sion that the date of its deposit lies well within the limits of the Dionysian period.

From the fact, already noticed, that many of the dies used were cracked and oxidized, and that nearly all the chief known varieties of "medallions," both by Kimôn and Evænetos, were represented in the hoard, it is evident that their issue had gone on for a considerable period of years before the date of its deposit. In a succeeding section I hope to show that the earliest Syracusan dekadrachms were first struck during the years that immediately succeeded the Athenian siege, those of Evænetos beginning about 406 B.C. This artist had already, at an earlier date, perhaps as early as 425 B.C., engraved tetradrachms in an earlier "manner" for the Syracusan mint. If we allow another score of years for the period of his later activity, which also shows a marked development in style, his latest "medallion" dies would reach down approximately to 385 B.C. It is, however, by no means impossible that the dies of both Kimôn and Evænetos may have been used for some time at least after those artists had ceased their activity; and the state to which some of the dies used for the coins of the present deposit had been reduced may be held to favour this view.

On the other hand, however, the absence from this hoard of Siculo-Punic tetradrachms of the later types imitated from Evænetos' "medallions," which are otherwise of constant occurrence in this as well as other parts of Sicily, is a significant fact. The coins of Hêrakleia Minôa (Rash Melkart) struck in the period immediately succeeding 383 B.C., when Dionysios restored it to the Carthaginians, show that soon after that date these Punic copies of Evænetos' head of Korê and the accompanying quadriga had become the usual types of

E

Carthaginian Sicily. That "Camp coins" with these types had been struck at Panormos or elsewhere at a somewhat earlier period than the autonomous issues of Rash Melkart is undeniable, and there seem to be good grounds for believing that the introduction of the type of Evænetos' Persephonê, on the coins struck by Carthage for her Sicilian mercenaries, was part of the atonement for the violation of the Syracusan sanctuary of " The Goddesses " by the troops of Himilkôn in 395 B.C.[10] The absence of any specimen of this abundant Siculo-Punic class from the present hoard makes it difficult to bring down the date of its deposit many years later than 380 B.C.

Hoards of coins may be divided into two main categories —those, namely, which represent the character of the local currency at the moment of their burial, and those the accumulation of which has been more gradual, and which, therefore, represent selections from the current coinage of a more or less extended period of years. It is to this latter class that the present find unquestionably belongs. Many of the coins found in this deposit, which are, typologically, the earliest, such as, for instance, the "medallions" in Kimôn's first style of low relief, are, nevertheless, among the best preserved. It is evident that in this hoard we have the savings of some individual put by year by year, and the comparative state of preservation of the different types contained in it does not, therefore, supply us with the same chronological data that would have been derived from a hoard of the other kind.

---

[10] Cf L. Müller, *Numismatique de l'ancienne Afrique*, ii., pp. 110, 111.

PART III

A DEKADRACHM BY A NEW ARTIST.

THE great prize of the Santa Maria hoard remains, however, to be described. This is the dekadrachm (fig. 1, p. 30) of which a phototype, enlarged to twice the diameter, appears on Plate IV.

The obverse exhibits the head of Persephonê to the left, wreathed with barley-leaves, and with four dolphins playing around as in Evænetos' well-known design. The present type, however, differs in important particulars from all known examples of Evænetos' handiwork. The face of the Goddess as here seen, beautiful as it is, reveals her to us in a new and severer aspect. The quadriga on the reverse, and the panoply below it, appear on a grander scale, and upon both sides of the coin the inscription is differently arranged. A careful analysis of the design, both on the obverse and reverse of this superb "medallion," shows divergences of style and execution that betray a different hand. The microscopic delicacy of the engraving on the present coin is indeed alone sufficient to place it in a category apart, and a minute comparison, which I had the advantage of making in Mr. Head's company, between this piece and the fine series of dekadrachms from the hand of Evænetos in the British Museum, convinced us both that the newly discovered "medallion" could not be the work of that artist during any period of his activity.

The eyes of the Maiden Goddess, as portrayed for us on the present coin, are longer in proportion to their height[1] and rendered more in accordance with the earlier tradition. The angle at which the upper and lower eyelids meet is less than in the case of Evænetos' work, the pupil of the eye is somewhat smaller and, except where slightly cut by the line of the upper eyelid, visible in its entirety, in contradistinction to those of the other artist, which are always more or less in profile.

In these respects the proportions of the eye show a greater affinity to those observed by the engraver Kimôn in his dekadrachms exhibiting the head of Arethusa in high relief. The present delineation is, however, of unrivalled delicacy. Both the pupil and iris are indicated with microscopic fineness, and the upper line of the under eyelid reveals a peculiarity which at once links it on to the work of the earlier Syracusan masters, as distinguished from that of the later school represented by Evænetos. In the age preceding the date of the engraver Eumenês[2] the under eyelashes were often fully reproduced. Eumenês himself at times reduced them to a mere line of dots, and after

---

[1] The length of the upper eyelid is 0·36 mill. as compared with 0·25 mill., the approximate average on fine signed coins of Evænetos. The length of the lower is 0·25 mill. as compared with 0·20 mill. The height of the eye itself is 0·14 mill. as compared with about 0·16. On the other hand the proportions of the eyes on the new "medallion" almost exactly tally with those of Kimôn's Arethusa head on his dekadrachms of high relief. These Kimônian dimensions may be approximately given as 0·35 mill. for the length of the upper eyelid, 0·25 for that of the lower, and 0·15 for the height of the eye between the upper and lower lids.

[2] For this form of the name see p. 60.

his time they disappear from the Syracusan dies. Beneath
the eye of Korê, however, as she is here depicted, the
lashes are still traceable in a series of minute punctuations,
so finely engraved on the upper edge of the lid that they
are only visible to ordinary sight with the aid of a strong
lens.

The nose is more purely "Grecian" and free from the
slight incurving at its spring that characterizes Evænetos'
profiles, both early and late.   It is more delicately
modelled, and shows no trace of that slight heaviness
about the nostrils that always somewhat weights the beautiful face of the Goddess as she appears on the rival dies.
The outline of the neck flows in a softer undulation ; the
bow of the chin is not so full.   The lips are more crisply
cut, and a prouder, perchance a sadder, expression hovers
about their corners.   It is as if the fatal pomegranate-seed
had passed them and left its taste of immortal bitterness. In
proportion to the module of the coin the maximum relief
is a shade lower,[3] but the locks of hair, the ear and corn-
wreath are, nevertheless, more deeply engraved.   The
curving spikes and folded sheaths of the barley-spray are
themselves rendered with greater fulness and naturalistic
detail.

But besides these more subtle discrepancies which
reveal themselves on a minute analysis of the type before
us, there are other differences in arrangement and design
that must strike the most casual observer.   The inscription ΣYPAKOΣIΩN, which on all other coins of this
class surrounds the upper part of Persephonê's head, is

---

[3] The greatest relief of the head is in this case 0·29 mille-
metre above the flat surface of the coin.   In the case of a fine
dekadrachm of Evænetos in the British Museum (with the inscription Δ) the relief is 0·33 mill.

here with fine artistic instinct transferred to the lower circumference of the coin, thus occupying the space reserved by Evænetos for his signature on some of his dekadrachms. The field is thus set free for a new and luxuriant development of "the Maiden's" curling tresses, which flow upwards and outwards, and seem "to wanton in Sicilian air," while others twine like bindweed about the curving spikes of the corn-blades. Beneath and in front are the usual four dolphins which define the

Fig. 1.—"Medallion" by New Artist.

character of the young Earth Goddess here as Lady of Ortygia—in a wider sense, perhaps, as Lady of the Isle of Sicily—but the ampler field around has enabled the artist in this case to endow them with fuller and more graceful forms, and thus to introduce minute naturalistic details such as the double ring round the eye-socket. They are as nearly as possible one-third larger than the dolphins on Evænetos' dies,[4] and the lower of the four is placed in immediate contact with the section of Persephonê's neck, so that it seems to bear up her head.

---

[4] The average maximum breadth of the dolphins' bodies on this coin is 0·28 mill. as compared with an average of about 0·19 mill. on signed dekadrachms of Evænetos. The average length is 1·36 mill. as compared with 1·25 mill.

The reverse type of this remarkable "medallion" stands equally apart from other coins of the same class. We have here, indeed, as upon the ordinary dekadrachm dies, the victorious quadriga and the panoply below, but we see them in a new and grander aspect, and with important variations in the character of the inscription and the design.

It cannot be denied that in the disposition of the horses' hind legs upon the dekadrachms of Evænetos there is an element of discord. They intersect one another at broken intervals, and in every variety of the design an ungraceful feature is supplied by two hind-legs of the second horse being placed on the ground together, an arrangement which is besides an impossible one, since it involves a prolongation of the horse itself to over half its natural length, while the foremost horse, on the contrary, is unduly shortened. In the action of the team, moreover, there is perceptible a tendency towards that sensationalism which is so characteristic of the tetradrachm types by the same artist, with their tangled and trailing reins, broken chariot wheels, and overset goals.

On the newly-discovered piece, on the other hand, though the distance between the fore and hind-legs of the foremost horse is still too small, the scheme as a whole is severely controlled within the limits of sobriety and harmony. The horses step together in perfect rhythm as if to the music of some stately pæan, and it is less the straining of the racer that is here portrayed for us than the crowned victor's measured course. The steeds themselves are of full and noble build, and entirely free from that slight attenuation of body which is the defect of Evænetos' more agitated compositions. They impress us with an overpowering sense of largeness altogether disproportionate to the field that holds them. We seem to be surveying a reduction of some great work of bronze or marble, and indeed it would be hard to match the blended power and beauty of the group before us outside the Parthenôn frieze.

A new feature is supplied in the present design, of which there is no trace on any known dekadrachm. This is the appearance beneath the forepart of the second horse of an angular ridge, the continuation of which may be traced above its head.[5] The effect produced in a perpendicular direction is identical with that exhibited below horizontally by the steps on which the arms are set out, and gives the spectator the appearance of a corner of masonry rather than of an Ionic column, such as by the analogy of other Sicilian coins we should expect were this intended to indicate the goal. It is further to be observed that, as the horses ran against the sun, the goal would have been on the left, which is here the nearer side.[6] It would seem therefore that the ridge in the background here represents the angle of a monument that overlooked the course and the extremity of which, here represented, marked the winning-line on the side opposite to that on which stood the columnar goal. It is from the summit of the erection thus indicated that Nikê flies forward to crown the charioteer, and it seems possible that we have here an indication of a stand on which the judges sat who decided on the issue of the race, Victory herself, whose statue, perhaps, crowned the whole, here standing for the more mortal arbiters of the contest.

---

[5] This continuation of the line above the horse's head shows that this feature in the design is intentional, and that it cannot be referred to a mere flaw in the die.

[6] As, for instance, on the reverse of a tetradrachm of Katanê, signed by Evænetos (*B. M. Cat.* No. 35).

In this connexion it will be remembered that on more than one ancient monument—some coins of Elis and Terina may be taken as numismatic examples—Nikê is seen perched aloft on a base or cippus, and the explanation of this may probably be seen in a design on a beautiful red-figured vase found at Chiusi, the main subject of which is a wrestling match between two youths.[7] Here Victory is seen seated above on a high basis or "stand" watching the match below, and evidently in the position of the umpire.

Another feature in which the present design differs from that of all other known dekadrachms is to be seen in the perfectly horizontal position of the goad held by the charioteer, the further end of which is hidden behind the horses' heads. In every other case the goad is held aslant, its upper portion visible above the horses' heads. Its level aim on the coin before us harmonizes well with the even action of the team itself, and seems to regulate their perfect time.

The arrangement of the reins again essentially differs from that adopted by Evænetos, and presents a much closer agreement with that of Kimôn. On Kimôn's dekadrachms, which present the particularity of exhibiting the up-turned end of the chariot pole, the nearer rein ascends and forks into two bridles, one on either side of the nearer horse's head.. Two reins are seen across the necks of the two central horses, while the outermost horse on the farther side of the quadriga is controlled like the first by a single bridle on either side. On Evænetos' dekadrachms the reins radiate more slightly from the hand of the charioteer; of these all four cross the neck of the nearest horse, three that of the second, two of the third,

---

[7] In the Ashmolean Museum at Oxford.

F

while the farthest horse is governed, on the side visible to the spectator, by a single rein which passes over the necks of all the others—a remarkable arrangement, which was doubtless resorted to in order to secure a greater control of the horses in rounding the goal.[8] It is obvious that at that critical point in the course a greater pull is required on the two outermost horses, which would have a tendency to fly off at a tangent, and this additional hold on them was apparently gained by passing the reins over the breasts of the two inner horses, so that they served as a kind of living pulley to the outermost. It is the moment of turning that Evænetos has here depicted for us. The outermost steed, pricked by the goad, springs forward, wheeling to the left, while with his left hand the charioteer draws in the reins so as to pull round the nearer horses.

In the case of the New "Medallion," on the other hand, we find, as already observed, that the arrangement of the reins differs entirely from that adopted by Evænetos on his dekadrachms,[9] while showing a closer agreement with that of Kimón. The reins here start straight and level from the driver's hands, while a single rein runs across the neck of each, dividing into two before it reaches the horse's bit. The horses themselves step together, and the horizontally extended goad well indicates that all is now straightforward. It is no longer the turning in the course that we have before us here. It is victorious arrival.

---

[8] Since this was written I notice that the same explanation had occurred to the Duc de Luynes (*Ann. dell' Inst.* 1830, p. 86).

[9] On his tetradrachms (which are of a decidedly earlier date than his dekadrachms) Evænetos conforms to the arrangement found on the new dekadrachm. This arrangement was in fact the usual one, both on coins and other monuments of this period.

Equal distribution and even-handed government cha-
racterise the whole of this noble composition. On the
other hand, the treatment of the horses' manes affords a
strong piece of internal evidence that this magnificent
design is from the graver of the same artist who executed
the luxuriant tresses of Persephonê as she appears upon
the obverse of our "medallion." While upon all the
hitherto-known dekadrachms by Evænetos and Kimôn
the manes of the horses are regular and close-cropped,
they are here seen curling upwards over the horses' fore-
heads and toss about their necks in waving locks. The
hair of the charioteer also attains a new development and
streams behind him in the breeze.

The prize armour in the exergue is exhibited in its
entirety. It is of larger make than that of the known dekadrachm types, it differs in arrangement, and presents a
greater variety of detail. The shield is broader and more
shapely. The crest of the helmet rises over the exergual
line; its upper part is decorated with a kind of *anthêmion*,
and its check-piece exhibits a relief, apparently a seated
Sphinx. Sprays of foliage, perhaps of olive, run along the
sides of the greaves, and the front of the cuirass and border
of the shield show traces of ornament; the *thorax* is turned
to the left instead of to the right as on all other " medallions." The most striking divergence from the received
type is, however, to be seen in the legend ΑΘΛΑ, which,
instead of being relegated in small type to the narrow
space beneath the cuirass, in the very rare cases where
it is preserved at all,[10] is here inscribed in large letters

---

[10] Among fifteen more or less select dekadrachms of Evænetos
in the British Museum, the inscription ΑΘΛΑ is only legible
on a single specimen. In the Cabinet des Médailles at Paris,
which is especially rich in this department, the proportion is

across the open space above the shield. As a consequence of this arrangement the *thorax*, which on all other dekadrachm types occupies the exact centre of the space below the quadriga, is pushed somewhat to the right, the slight overweighting of that side of the exergue that might seem to ensue being skilfully counterbalanced by the angle of masonry that rises above the exergual line on the other side. Finally, in the corner behind the helmet are traces of what appears to be a small monogram somewhat resembling ⊢Κ or ΝΚ, with possibly another letter.

In this monogram we cannot hesitate to seek the name of the engraver of the "medallion" itself. Unfortunately, it is not clear enough on the coin to supply a certain reading, but so much may be regarded as certain that no ingenuity can connect it with the name of Evænetos.

The minute analysis of the design already given has enabled us to detect such an array of divergencies, alike in style and detail, from all the known works of Evænetos, that even without the signature we should be justified in concluding that the die of this remarkable dekadrachm was executed by another hand. That slight varieties exist among the dekadrachm dies of the rival artists is of course well known. But amongst all these variations, certain fixed limits are laid down which are never overpassed. The place of the legend on both obverse and reverse, the eyes, profile, and expression of the Goddess, the general arrangement of her hair, of the reins and goad in the hands of the charioteer, the distribution of the legs

---

about the same. On the remaining dekadrachms of the Santa Maria hoard it was only preserved in two examples—one on a coin by Evænetos (Pl. V., fig. 12), and the other, but imperfectly, on a coin signed by Kimón.

of the horses, their cropped manes and the absence of the perpendicular ridge behind, the character and position of the armour in the exergue—these are so many constant features on the whole series of Evænetos' "medallions" every one of which is set aside in the present instance.

It might, perhaps, be argued, on the other hand, that we have here a record of an attempt of Evænetos' great rival and contemporary, the engraver Kimôn, to excel him in his own chosen subject, the head of the youthful Goddess, or that we have here from Kimôn's hands the original of the type which Evænetos afterwards made his own. Attention has already been called to certain features in which the obverse head of the newly discovered piece shows a distinct sympathy with Kimôn's style of portraiture. The eye and profile of Persephonê as here delineated, the dolphin below her neck and the folds of the neck itself, are all Kimônian. The extreme delicacy and minuteness of the work is more nearly approached by some of Kimôn's earliest dekadrachms of lower relief than by any of Evænetos. The flowing locks of the Goddess may themselves recall the facing head of Arethusa by the former artist. Upon the reverse, again, the arrangement of the reins corresponds with that on Kimôn's dies. The figure of the flying Nikê betrays the same affinity.

It must, however, be borne in mind, that all the known *pentêkontalitra* from the hand of this engraver are associated on the obverse with the head of Arethusa, and that all are signed both on the obverse and reverse. The reverse signatures, moreover, are all in full on the exergual line, and neither the method nor position corresponds with the present example. In the monogram—if monogram it be—on the New "Medallion" a **K** indeed apparently occurs, but it does not seem to be the initial letter, and the abbreviated forms of Kimôn's signature known to us are either a single **K** or **KI** or **KIM**.

The chariot and horses again here presented differ as radically from those on any known dekadrachm of Kimôn as from those of Evænetos. Kimôn's reverse types are indeed unvarying. From his earliest " medallion " with the head in low relief to his latest work in high relief, we have the same scheme of the quadriga, two of the horses of which have their hinder pair of legs placed together on the ground, a scheme which is the starting point of Evænetos' types, who, however, diminishes the ungainliness of the effect by confining himself to a single pair in this position.[11] How different from this is the rhythmic movement of the horses' legs on the new "medallion"! It is inconceivable that an artist who had once hit on a design so beautiful and harmonious should have reverted to such a comparatively crude and ungraceful scheme. If we turn again to the panoply below, it will be seen that Kimôn's arrangement answers in every respect to that adhered to by Evænetos. The cuirass is placed in the centre, the shield and helmet balanced against each other, while the **ΑΘΛΑ** is transferred to the lowest exergual space in small letters. The armour itself is of comparatively diminutive size, and the cuirass is turned to the right.

On the whole, then, in spite of some sympathies exhibited in the style, we are reduced to the conclusion that

---

[11] It is observable, however, that whereas Kimôn's scheme is, so far as it goes, a possible arrangement and is reconcileable with the horses' dimensions, that of Evænetos is impossible, and requires us to stretch the body of the second horse to half an additional length (see p. 31). The motive of the hind legs set together on the ground is simply a *survival* from the Archaic and early Transitional coin-types.

there is no warrant for regarding the present " medallion " as the work of Kimôn any more than of Evænetos. We have no alternative left but to recognise in this master-piece of artistic skill the work of a new and hitherto unknown engraver of the dekadrachm dies of Syracuse. The work itself stands apart from the tradition alike of Kimôn and Evænetos, and represents an independent essay of the highest merit in this branch of numismatic art.

It will, nevertheless, be observed that the fine head of Persephonê on the present coin stands in a very close relation to Evænetos' rendering of the same subject. Up to a certain point one artist has copied from the other. The same is true with regard to certain features on the reverse, and notably the introduction of the armour grouped on the steps beneath the chariot.

The interesting questions remain—To whom is due the original—at least, so far as concerns numismatic art—of this exquisite type of the young Goddess ? By which of the two artists was first suggested the magnificent com-bination of the prize arms with the victorious quadriga ? In other words, must the issue of the piece before us be regarded as earlier or later than that of the first deka-drachms of Evænetos ?

In this connexion it becomes important to consider in what relation the present dekadrachm stands to Syracusan types of the earliest period of the signed coinage, and that immediately preceding it.

The luxuriant development of Persephonê's hair is, as already noticed, somewhat suggestive of Kimôn's master-piece, the facing head of Arethusa (Pl. III., 4, 5). The flowing curls of our coin find also a certain analogy in the tetradrachms of Eukleidas, struck about the year 415 B.C., which apparently portray the nymph Arethusa diving down into her pool with her tresses streaming upwards. A ruder but in some respects still nearer precedent is, however, supplied by a tetradrachm type from the hand of the older master Eumenês, in which a female head is seen bound round twice with a cord, while above and below loose curling tresses flow out from the whole crown of the head.

Fig. 2.—Head, by Eumenês.

In the evolution of the head of Persephonê upon the dekadrachm before us, this earlier type has evidently played a part, and the incurving of the lower part of the back hair is itself a decorative "survival" of the impress made upon it by the cord that confined it on the earlier design. The upper boundary of this cluster of hair is again marked by a depression which represents the channel, if such a term is applicable, of the second cord that confines the back tresses of the prototype. The upper line of the cord, moreover, as it crosses the top of the head, seems actually to suggest the line followed by the uppermost spike of the barley-wreath on the deka-drachm.

The Syracusan coin types grow; they are not, as a rule, invented off-hand and without reference to pre-existing monetary traditions. Great as is the advance on the ruder work of Eumenês and other older artists exhibited by the noble dekadrachm types, surpassing as was the

artistic skill with which the earlier details were absorbed
and transformed into what, to the unhistoric observer,
may seem purely original compositions, traces may yet
be found in their beautiful and harmonious lines of the
older elements out of which they were evolved.

The head of Arethusa as she appears on Kimôn's fifty-
litra pieces may be traced back in the same way as the
design before us to a traditional type handed on by Eumenês
to his successors[12]. Taken in connexion with the tetradrachm head by the same Eumenês, exhibiting a perfect
halo of curling tresses, the effigy of Korê as she appears on
the newly discovered "medallion" has for us a new interest,
as supplying, as it were, an intermediate link between this
older creation and the head of the Goddess as she appears
on the well-known dekadrachm series of Evænetos. And
so far as the present type shows a greater approach to this
pre-existing design, so far it supplies us with an argument
for regarding it as anterior in development and date to
the dekadrachm heads of Evænetos. If this conclusion
be correct, we must suppose that Evænetos restored the
civic inscription to its more usual place around the head,
at the cost of some of Korê's superabundant tresses. In
the treatment of the eye, again, as already pointed out,
the better perspective of Evænetos' rendering represents
a distinctly later stage of artistic development. The
purer Greek profile, and the comparatively large size of
the dolphins on the new "medallion," are also characteristic of an earlier period.

The inference to which we are thus led by an internal
analysis of the obverse type of our dekadrachm, that it
represents rather the original than the copy of the head

---

[12] See p. 54 *seqq.*

G

of the Korê, as she appears on the parallel coinage of Evænetos, is strongly reinforced by a consideration of the reverse design of the same piece. Here we have to deal with a simpler and grander form of the quadriga, which typologically at least, is certainly anterior to that associated with Evænetos' handiwork. The action of the horses in this case is altogether free from that sensational element which characterizes the signed dekadrachms of Evænetos, and which, during the years that preceded Dionysios' dictatorship, was rapidly gaining momentum on the Sicilian dies. It is strange indeed that the same artist who, in his head of Persephonê, may be said to trespass on the domain of painting, should on the other side of the same piece have executed what is unquestionably the most sculpturesque and monumental of all the Syracusan coin-types. Yet, as already shown, there are certain points of sympathy between the obverse and reverse designs, such as notably the free treatment of the horses' manes, which tend to show that, as in the case of all known dekadrachms, both sides of the coin are by the same hand. The abandonment of the regular close-cropped type of mane, such as is seen in the Pheidiac school of sculpture, in favour of a naturalistic rendering, is so far as it goes an advanced characteristic and an anticipation of one of the finest features of the horses on the Fourth-Century Tarentine Coinage; a similar tendency is, however, already seen on the noble dekadrachms of Akragas, struck before 406 B.C. The fuller and less attenuated forms of the horses recall those of the Akragantine engraver MYP,[13] who seems to have

---

[13] *B. M. Cat.*, *Agrigentum*, 53, 54. There is an excellent reproduction of this type in Weil, *Die Künstlerinschriften der sicilischen Münzen*, Taf. i. 13.

flourished during the years that immediately preceded
406 B.C., the date of the destruction of that city. As
compared with the other dekadrachm types of Syracuse,
their proportions are more in keeping with the canon of
Kimôn, whose earliest "medallions," as I hope to show in
the succeeding section, are somewhat anterior in date to
those of Evænetos. On the other hand, there exist some
early reverse types of dekadrachms by the latter artist [14]
in which the action of the horses is less agitated than in
his usual scheme, and which, perhaps, supply the nearest
attainable comparison to the quadriga on the present coin,
though the disposition of the horses' legs on Evænetos'
designs suffers from the usual defects, and both the bearing and proportions of the steeds on the Santa Maria
type are very distinctly nobler. The influence of the
New Artist on Evænetos seems to be distinctly traceable
in these pieces.

The more intimate relations in which, upon the newly
discovered *pentêkontalitron*, the steps and panoply below
stand to the quadriga above, afford a further and most
important argument for the anteriority of the present
type. On the "medallions" alike of Kimôn and Evænetos,
the exergual arrangements appear as mere subsidiary
details. The pictorial schemes of the chariot and horses
above have no need for an architectural base on which to
support them. But the presentation of the quadriga by
the New Artist is, as we have seen, of a very different
character. It is wholly monumental, and at once suggests
the fact that the artist had in his mind's eye some individual *anathêma*, either in bronze or marble. The steps
corroborate this view, and may be taken actually to repre-

---

[14] Cf. especially Pl. V., fig. 10.

sent the graduated base of a monument in every way appropriate to a hippodrome, and upon which the arms that served as prizes in the contest were actually placed.

When too on the dekadrachms by the other artists we find the steps and armour below dwindling down to mere ornamental appendages, and the horses above showing action of a kind suggesting rather the freedom of a painter's brush, we have good grounds for supposing that the scheme on our present " medallion," in which the plastic character of the chariot group and the graduated base below mutually explain one another, is the earlier design.

The fuller and more realistic presentation of the armour, as well as the prominence of the inscription that indicates its destination as the prize of victory, taken by themselves supply some grounds for seeing in this part of the design as it appears in the New " Medallion" the original of the exergual arrangement that was adopted in a modified and more decorative form by Kimôn, and after him by Evænetos, upon their dekadrachm dies.

The technical peculiarities of the present piece which mark it off, not less distinctly than its originality of style and design, from all other coins of this class, point on the whole to the same conclusion. The relief, both on the obverse and reverse, is somewhat lower than that on Evænetos' " medallions," and shows a nearer approach to that of Kimôn's earlier work. Its quadriga especially reveals a more shallow intaglio of the die, recalling the finest Fifth-Century style of gem-engraving. The mechanical skill with which this coin has been struck is truly remarkable. A slight reduplication of lines may indeed be detected round the outermost rim of the obverse, but I know of no dekadrachm that can compare with this, either in the roundness of the circumference, or in the precision with which the impression of the die on either side has been centred on the metal, so that not only is the whole design, both on the obverse and reverse, contained within the field, but in neither case is there a lopsided margin. The module of the coin is abnormally large, being 1·51 inch (3·84 mill.) or ·06 inch broader than the largest "medallion" of Evænetos in the British Museum. In its exceptional module the present coin unquestionably ranges better with the dekadrachms from the hand of Kimôn, amongst which the average expanse is decidedly greater than on those by Evænetos. Amongst the specimens in the British Museum, there are two of Kimôn's work, the modules of which reach respectively 1·55 and 1·6 inch, and a third "medallion" of the same artist (with the lower relief) in the collection of the University of Aberdeen measures 1·55. And inasmuch as Kimôn's first dekadrachm issues belong to a slightly earlier date than those of Evænetos,[15] the abnormally large module of the piece by the New Artist must also tell in favour of its comparatively early date. The Akragantine dekadrachms, which are also relatively early, range between 1·46 inch (3·7 mill.) and 1·62 inch (4·1 mill.).[16]

Were there any trace of a progressive diminution in the weight of Syracusan silver money during this period, the decidedly light weight of this exceptional dekadrachm which weighs 645½ grains, as against an average of over 665 grains, might be taken as distinct evidence of posteriority of issue. But there is no trace of such a progressive diminution, and on the other hand a considerable varia-

---

[15] See Parts IV. and V.
[16] Salinas, *Le Monete delle antiche Città di Sicilia*, p. 21.

tion in weight is perceptible in known examples of Evænetos' dekadrachms, one in the British Museum descending as low in the scale as 650 grains. Undoubtedly for a coin which, with the exception of the loss of a few small flakes of silver in the upper field of the reverse, is brilliantly preserved, and of extraordinary large module, a discrepancy of some 20 grains is a noteworthy phenomenon. In the case, however, of a dekadrachm by Kimôn in the British Museum, the authenticity of which there seems no good reason for doubting, and which is by no means in bad condition, the weight falls as low as 625·3 grains.[17]

The general conclusion, then, to which these various lines of induction seem to point is that the newly discovered "medallion" is slightly earlier in date than any known dekadrachm from the hand of Evænetos. In that case the unknown artist with whom we have to deal was in all probability the original creator of the beautiful type of the young Goddess crowned with the green barley-wreath of Spring, which, in a slightly modified form, was reproduced and popularized on the prolific issues of Evænetos.

It is possible, indeed—and this perhaps is the preferable view—that the reverse type as seen on the new "medallion," which seems to betray a less developed style than the obverse head, was originally coupled with a still earlier version of the head of Korê than that with which it is actually associated. The fact that the present coin is altogether unique, and the possibility, therefore, that it was struck for some special purpose connected with the

---

[17] *B. M. Cat., Syracuse*, No. 203. It has the same flaw in the die as another piece of full weight.

prize of an agonistic contest, make it reasonable to suppose that a still earlier, but hitherto undiscovered, version
of the obverse type may yet lie behind it. In this case,
the head of Persephonê that it exhibits would represent
a parallel development of an original model, used also by
Evænetos, rather than the original model itself. The
perspective rendering of the spiral curls on the new
"medallion" is seen on Kimôn's early dies in a more
incipient stage, and is conspicuous by its absence on his
facing head of Arethusa. On the "medallions" of
Evænetos, on the other hand, this artistic feature is seen
in much the same stage of development, though the curls
of his Korê are still more closely coiled; and this fact
may be taken to supply an argument for bringing down
the execution of the obverse design of the New Artist
approximately to the same date as the early "medallions"
of Evænetos. In any case, however, the early characteristics observable both on the obverse and reverse of our
coin make it difficult to suppose that it is merely a later
copy based on Evænetos' design.

The discovery of the present "medallion" is in other
respects of high interest in the history of the glyptic art
as affording us a new stand-point of comparison for the
well-known masterpiece from the hand of Evænetos.
The relation in which the coin before us stands to it
has already been generally indicated. In many respects
the contrast only serves to bring into clearer relief the
peculiar charms of each. The New Engraver excels in
minute elaboration of details, but his presentment of the
Maiden Goddess, though richer in accessories, is severer
in profile and nobler in expression. The portrait by
Evænetos, on the other hand, is a work of greater artistic
concentration. The details are better subordinated to

the general effect. Quite secondary attention is here
paid to the background. The cutting-off of the super-
fluous tresses brings out the fine outline of the head
itself and throws the whole into greater relief, while the
slighter rendering of the surrounding dolphins also
serves to give greater prominence to the central design.
Their curves are balanced against the outlines of the face
and neck with calculated skill, the bowed outline of the
lowermost dolphin, for example, no longer following, and
almost repeating the line of the neck-section immediately
above, but standing here in accentuated contrast to its more
gentle sweep, while the flowing inner bend formed by the
upper of the two fish in front of Korê's face intensifies, by
the law of opposition, the soft incurving of the line that
unites her nose and forehead, and which breaks the
classical severity of profile.

The eye in Evænetos' portrait is, as we have seen,
in better perspective. The modelling of the ear and
cheek is executed with greater ease and truth to nature,
and about the corners of the lips there lurks a very human
dimple. It is a girlish face, rather Greuze-like in its
expression, and of surpassing loveliness, that we have
before us from Evænetos' dies, but something of the
diviner element that permeates the earlier impersonation
seems here to have faded from our view.

If we turn to the reverse of the newly discovered dekadrachm, while we admire the simplicity and grandeur of
the quadriga group, with its rhythmic and harmonious
movement, we cannot fail to notice, at the same time, a
certain naïveness and uniformity in the arrangement. In
spite of the admirable modulation of movement the drawing
is somewhat too regular. The goad and outstretched arm,
the reins, the axle-tree, and steps below, all form a series

of parallel lines, and the horses—all equally controlled
and equidistant—in the bearing of their heads and necks
and the arrangement of their legs, repeat the same action.
The quadriga types of Evænetos, on the other hand,
especially as seen in the maturity of their development
on such a piece as that represented on Plate V., Fig. 12,
betray throughout a hand that has spent a long appren-
ticeship in the art of design. The composition itself,
which suggests, without actually showing, the moment of
rounding the goal, is of unrivalled ingenuity. The action
of the horses is higher and incomparably more varied.
The raised goad, the more radiating reins and their
adroitly devised arrangement, the rearing horses, the disposal of the legs into two distinct groups, are all so many
evidences of freehanded striving after a magnificent
and elaborately calculated artistic effect. If the other
design runs on monumental lines, that of Evænetos might
translate itself into a painter's masterpiece. It is only
when we analyse the scheme more carefully that we see
that the arrangement, striking and effective as it seems,
has yet its defects; that the two hind-legs of the second
horse placed on the ground imply a body dispropor-
tionately long, that the hind-legs of the foremost horse
would make (as in the other instance) a body dispropor-
tionately short, and that the complex crossing of the legs
themselves, that adds variety and sensation to the design,
is fatal to the harmony and dignity that shine in the older
composition.

The arrangement of the panoply and inscription below
on Evænetos' coin certainly lacks nothing in regard to
symmetry, and the transference of the inscription ΑΘΛΑ
in minute letters to the lowest exergual space is, from this
point of view, a neat device. But this nicely balanced

grouping of the arms with their triple ascending scale is, after all, a paltry set-off against the massive simplicity of the older design. How poor are the shield and helmet, the greaves and cuirass, by comparison ! How shrunken from their heroic mould ! The perfect equipoise achieved, itself contributes to reduce them almost to an ornamental appendage of the quadriga above, and like the legend that describes them, their meaning as the prize of a great agonistic contest stands out no longer bold and clear as on the earlier piece. As a matter of fact on over ninety per cent. of these later "medallions" as actually struck, the ΑΘΛΑ below is entirely lost.

In examining the handiwork of Evænetos we cannot fail to recognise at every turn the characteristics of a more advanced art, and yet with all the trained artistic skill and brilliant power of composition displayed by this engraver, with all the beauty of his portraiture, it must still be acknowledged that in delicacy of touch and majesty of design he stands behind the earlier Master whose splendid work has been now revealed to us. The coin itself, with its infinite refinement of execution, with its alternating moods of picturesque luxuriance and sculpturesque majesty, is a *tour de force* which may, perhaps, be compared with some of the medallic master-pieces of the Italian Renascence executed by artists whose main lines ran along the higher paths of painting, sculpture, and architecture.

PART IV.

THE DEKADRACHMS OF KIMÔN, AND HIS PLACE ON THE SYRACUSAN DIES.

REASONS have been given in the preceding section for regarding the newly-discovered "medallion" from the Santa Maria hoard as of somewhat earlier fabric than any known dekadrachm of Evænetos. The severe and simple style of the reverse has even inclined us to go a step farther, and to regard its most characteristic feature, the prize arms ranged on the steps below the chariot, as representing the original type from which both Kimôn and Evænetos drew for their less striking and more conventionalized representation of the same subject.

The fact that the coin of the New Artist exhibits the reverse design in this naïve and independent form at least tends to show that the die was engraved, broadly speaking, in the earliest period of the revived *pentēkontalitra* and before the otherwise universal arrangement of the exergual arms had, as it were, become stereotyped.

Judging, however, by its obverse side, which apparently represents a later element on the new coin, a certain priority must be accorded to Kimôn's earlier Syracusan work, described above as Types I. and II. The epigraphy on the new "Medallion" no longer shows the transitional И that characterizes Kimôn's two earlier types, and on the other hand the formation of the eye, the arrangement of the lowermost dolphin and the style of relief show a greater sympathy with Kimôn's Third Type. On the whole then we may regard the head of Korê by the New Artist as contemporary with this.

It must at the same time be observed that there are certain features in the design of the unique piece from the Santa Maria hoard, which throw a new light on this remarkable class of coins, and bring us a step nearer to determining their original meaning and occasion. It will be well, however, before entering on the more historic part of our inquiry to consider the materials for the chronology of the early dekadrachm issues of Syracuse supplied by the dies of the other artists. The materials for this study are to be found both in the contents of some recent Sicilian finds, and in a comparative examination of certain kindred types, both of Syracuse itself and of other cities, the importance of which in this connexion seems hitherto to have escaped notice, but which hold out a welcome clue to the date of these "medallions." And the inquiry thus embarked on may lead us, so far as Kimôn is concerned, to some new conclusions as to the position occupied by this artist among Sicilian engravers.

I am well aware that in ascribing a certain anteriority to Kimôn's dekadrachms as compared with those of Evænetos, I am advancing a proposition directly at variance with the opinion of one of the most careful and competent critics who have treated of the subject. Dr. Weil in his work on the artists' signatures on Sicilian coins, after dividing the dekadrachms with the head of Korê into an earlier class signed **EYAINE**, and a later unsigned, continues, "The third, and obviously the latest, class is that proceeding from Kimón and exhibiting the female head with the hair-net."[1] But Dr. Weil does not seem to have realised the existence of Kimón's earlier and rarer type, a phototype of which is given on Plate I., fig. 5,[2] and enlarged 2 diams. on Pl. VIII. The lower relief of the head of Arethusa on this coin, the incomparably finer engraving, and the truly exquisite elaboration of detail, stamp this at once as distinctly the earliest of Kimón's dekadrachms. It is evident, indeed, that some few years must have elapsed between this and his latest issue with the head of the same Nymph in bold relief—the proudest, and so far as its expression goes, the "modernest" of all Greek coin-types. Nor will any one with the earlier type in view seriously contest Kimón's claim to priority over his rival Evænetos in the engraving of dekadrachm dies.

These earliest "medallions" with Kimón's signature are of considerable rarity, though the Santa Maria hoard has

---

[1] Dr. Weil expresses himself (*Die Künstlerinschriften*, &c., p. 27) as follows: "Die Dekadrachmen scheiden sich in drei Gruppen, welche, soweit ich beobachten konnte, durch keinerlei Stempelvertauschungen unter einander in Beziehung stehen: die älteste ist die des Euainetos mit dem **EYAINE** unter dem Kopf des Kora; ihr in der Technik völlig entsprechend ist die statt des Künstlernamens mit wechselnden Beizeichen ausgestattete; die dritte und offenbar jüngste ist die von Kimon herrührende, der Frauenkopf mit dem Haarnetz." To these may now be added, besides the other and far rarer type of Arethusa by Kimón, the Korê head, by the New Artist, revealed to us by the Santa Maria hoard. Von Sallet, *Die Künstlerinschriften auf griechischen Münzen*, p. 29, is more cautious in expressing his opinion as to a possible difference in date between the two artists. He observes: "Ueber einen etwaigen, jedenfalls sehr geringen Zeitunterschied zwischen Kimon und Euänetos lässt sich nichts bestimmtes sagen."

[2] Cf. Castelli, *Sic. Vet. Num.*, Tav. lxxii. 2; Duc de Luynes, *Monumenti Inediti* (1830), Pl. XIX. 3, and *Annali dell' Inst.*, &c. (1830), pp. 77, 78; B. V. Head, *Coins of Syracuse*, Pl. IV. 6; *B. M. Cat., Sicily*, No. 200.

added two to our store of known specimens. The reverse, which is from the same die as that used in some of the later issues, shows the signature **KIMΩN** on the exergual line, but whereas on the obverse of the later types the full inscription of the name is repeated on the lowermost dolphin, it is here confined to the three letters $\begin{smallmatrix} KI \\ M \end{smallmatrix}$ inscribed on the *ampyx* of the *sphendonê*. The earlier **N** appears in the civic inscription.

If we examine the beautiful head of Arethusa on this coin, it becomes evident that it is itself a luxuriant and more elaborate adaptation of the head of the same Nymph as she appears on an early tetradrachm of Evænetos (Pl. I. fig. 3), while the quadriga type with which it is accompanied will also be found to stand in a very intimate relation to the reverse of the same piece by the rival master.

The tetradrachm in question is that finely executed coin[3] on which the first four letters of Evænetos' name appear on the belly of the dolphin that swims in front of the Nymph's mouth, while on the reverse the full signature is repeated in the earlier genitival form **EYAINETO** for **EYAINETOY** on a small tablet held aloft by Victory. Extraordinary as is this coin, regarded as an independent work of art, it is yet in many of its essential features itself simply an adaptation by the more skilful hand of the pupil from an existing model by the older master, Eumenês (Pl. I. fig. 1). At times, indeed, this older version of the head of Arethusa—if Arethusa it be—with the same starspangled sphendonê knotted at top in a similar manner, and the same arrangement of locks flowing back from the temple, appears with Eumenês' name below in actual association with the reverse of Evænetos (exhibiting his

---

[3] *B. M. Cat. Sicily*, p. 172, No. 188, *v. infra*, p. 85 *seqq.*

signature on the suspended tablet), which otherwise accompanies the younger engraver's more refined rendering of the obverse type.

This overlapping of Evænetos' fine design with the more archaic work of Eumenês is itself a clear indication of the early date of the tetradrachm in question. Nor is this by any means the only reason for assigning to this highly elaborate composition a very early place among the signed coins of Syracuse. Of the chronological importance of this coin in its bearings on the development of Syracusan art I have, indeed, already said something in connexion with a newly-discovered signature of an artist on one of the latest coins of Himera, the reverse of which was unquestionably copied from the tetradrachm of Evænetos.[4] In the paper in question I showed that not only was this late Himeræan type derived from Evænetos' model, but that from the more advanced character of the design we were justified in inferring that the prototype had been struck some years, at least, before 409 B.C., the latest assignable date for the tetradrachm of Himera.

This conclusion receives a striking corroboration from a beautiful tetradrachm of Segesta (Pl. I. fig. 4), presenting a head of the eponymous Nymph of that city unquestionably based on the Arethusa of the same early masterpiece of Evænetos. In this case, the head of Segesta can hardly be otherwise described than as an enlarged copy, in a more advanced style, of the Syracusan model. To this beautiful coin I shall have occasion to return when discussing the works of Evænetos.[5] Here it may be sufficient to say that there are good historical and numismatic grounds for referring its approximate date to the

---

[4] *Num Chron.*, 1890, p. 291 *seqq.*   [5] See p. 89 *seqq.*

years 416—413 B.C. The result, as will be seen, throws
back the prototype by Evænetos some years before this
date. Nor, allowing for the visible development in style
in the case of the Segestan coin, will it be safe to place
the date of issue of Evænetos' early tetradrachm many
years later than 425 B.C.

On the other hand, the great approximation in style
between the head of Segesta on the piece referred to, and
the Arethusa of Kimôn's early dekadrachm, affords in
this case, too, a valuable indication of date.

Both coins stand in much the same artistic relation to
the same prototype. In some respects, indeed, Kimôn in
his head of Arethusa shows a greater independence of his
model. The chin is fuller and rounder, and the nose and
forehead form more of a Grecian line ; in the character of
the eye and the general arrangement of the hair and *sphen-
donè* we find the same agreement, though on the larger coin
the curls are more developed, and here, in place of the star-
spangled bag, the back tresses, as on an earlier Syracusan
type (Pl. I., fig. 2), are confined in a beaded net which
supplies a greater richness and variety to the design. In
both cases the band that passes round the upper part of
the head is fastened by a small knot of the same form,
the loose ends of which curve above the head, Kimôn in
his arrangement of these streamers following rather the
prototype of Eumenês than Evænetos' adaptation of it.
On the whole, however, he has unquestionably developed
the model as refined by the latter artist, and in the
elaboration of detail and the almost microscopic minuteness of execution that Kimôn here displays there is much
in harmony with Evænetos' early manner as exhibited in
his head of Arethusa. One point, which is not without
its chronological importance, remains to be noticed. On

Kimôn's early medallion, as on the Segestan tetradrachm, there is substituted, in place of the coiled earrings that at Syracuse mark Transitional fashion, a new and more tasteful floral drop. As an additional token of contemporaneity and kinship this ornamental feature has a distinct value, inasmuch as amongst all the coins of the Sicilian cities this floral type of earring appears alone on these two pieces.

If we turn to the reverse of Kimôn's dekadrachm, there will also be observed a certain correspondence with that of Evænetos' early tetradrachm in the distribution of the foreparts of the horses. Here, as there, the three nearest horses are placed more or less abreast, while the further steed plunges forward. It is true, however, that—in deference, as has been suggested, to a severer model—the more sensational element of the design as represented by the broken rein and entangled fore-leg has been eliminated in Kimôn's scheme. On the other hand, the signature presents another point of contact between the two engravers. The practice adopted here by Kimôn of inscribing his name on the exergual line of the reverse is, in fact, adopted from another early tetradrachm reverse of Evænetos with an almost identical scheme of horses, in which his name, once more in the genitival form **EYAINETO**, is stowed away in the same manner. This reverse of Evænetos accompanies a head by his fellow-engraver Eukleidas which represents a copy contemporary with his own of the original portrait of Arethusa by their common master Eumenês.

Two Syracusan tetradrachms (figs. 6 and 7 of Pl. I.) may be referred to as illustrating much the same stage of artistic evolution as Kimôn's early dekadrachm. The first of these, with the head of the bearded Satyr beneath the Nymph's neck, shows the same indebtedness to

I

Evænetos' early model, the exceptional form of her ear-ring, on the other hand, being equally characteristic of the varied fashions in this matter displayed in Kimôn's day. The other coin, with the signature ΓΑΡΜΕ, while it also, in some respects, shows traces of the same proto-type, bears in a higher degree the impress of Kimôn's first "medallion" type, and has one motive directly borrowed from it, namely, the dolphin that seems to issue from Are-thusa's neck. Both these tetradrachms show a somewhat early chariot-scheme, in which the archaic dualism is well marked, and though somewhat later in style, neither can be many years later in date than Kimôn's first "medallion" type. His gold hundred-litra pieces (Pl. II., 3, 4, 9), with a head of Arethusa in the starry *sphendonê*, belong to the same group; and the facial type presented by the earliest of these (Pl. II, figs. 3, 4) so strongly recalls the features of Kimôn's second "medallion" issue (Type II.) that it must unquestionably be referred to the same date.[6]

From what has been already said, it will be seen that the earliest of Kimôn's "medallion" types fits on to the fine tetradrachm of Evænetos' "first manner," the head of which had already, between the approximate dates of 416 and 413 B.C., served as the model for the beautiful por-trait of Segesta on the rare tetradrachms of that city, while the tablet-holding Nikê of the reverse had already, by 409 B.C., been associated on a Himeræan coin with a quadriga scheme of a distinctly more advanced character. And the parallelism in which Kimôn's work stands to the Segestan coin referred to, is of such a kind as to warrant us in supposing that this early "medallion" dates from the same period as the other coin, and must be referred to the years immediately succeeding 415 B.C.

---

[6] See p. 93.

This conclusion, which carries back the prototype by Evænetos, and the contemporary types by Eukleidas and Eumenês, with which it stands in such close association, to a period which may be roughly stated as 425—415, has some important bearings on the chronology of Syracusan letter forms. On these early tetradrachms of Evænetos, the Ω appears already in the civic name, and the same is the case with the obverse types of the older engraver, Eumenês, which not infrequently accompany Evænetos' reverses. Nor need this conclusion, which throws back the first introduction of the Ω on the coin types of Syracuse to a considerably earlier date than has been generally supposed, in any way surprise us. There is no reason why Syracuse should have been behind any Italian city in such matters, and we know that at Thurii the Ω already appears on the earliest tetradrachms struck, in all probability, about 440 B.C. The Ω is in fact already used in his signatures by the Syracusan engraver Sôsiôn, on coins which go back approximately to the same date. There is then no *a priori* reason for supposing that the presence of the Ω on the group of coins with which we are immediately concerned, argues a later date than that to which their issue has been referred on other grounds. The earlier usage still lingered, indeed, at Syracuse itself, and some engravers lagged behind others in the introduction of the new letters. At times, too, they made use of them with an opposite force to that finally received. Eumenês himself, whose signature on his latest pieces EYMENOY shows the true form of his name, on slightly earlier coins, signs EYMHNOY—using H for E.[7] Phrygillos in the

---

[7] On his more archaic coins with the civic inscription ϞYPAKOϞION, this artist invariably signs EYMHNOY,

like fashion on' one occasion writes the civic name
ΣΥΡΑΚΩΣΙΟΝ—using Ω for O and *vice versâ*. So,
too, on a red-figured vase we find HPME[Σ] for EPMHΣ
and ΔΙΩΝΥΣΩΣ for ΔΙΟΝΥΣΟΣ.[8] Eukleidas is
more cautious about the new usage, and resorts to the
adjectival form ΣΥΡΑΚΟΣΙΟΣ. It seems to me that
this latter usage, which becomes so general just at this
period of epigraphic transition, was really a device for
avoiding any decision as to the force of the new letter-
forms.

One of the most valuable standpoints for fixing the date
of the Syracusan coin-types of this period is supplied by the
reverse design signed EYΘ (Pl. I. fig. 1), representing a
quadriga with horses in free but very even action, with
their fore-parts more turned towards the spectator than is
usual on this series, and driven by a winged youth. The
exergual device, a figure of Skylla chasing a small fish with
outstretched hand, is singularly sportive and graceful, but
the early date of the type seems to be established by its
exclusive association with the somewhat rude heads of
Korê and Arethusa, by Eumenês, and with a head of the
Maiden Goddess, by Phrygillos, after Eumenês' prototype,
which must certainly be regarded as the earliest work of
that engraver. It will be further observed that this
design presents an extraordinary parallelism with a similar
quadriga, also driven by a winged figure—in this case of
Nikê—that accompanies one of the latest tetradrachm

---

or $\frac{EYMH}{YON}$. On his later types associated with reverses by
Evænetos or Euth . . ., and with the inscription ΣΥΡΑΚΟΣ-
ΙΩΝ, the signature is always EYME[N]OY. This shows
that the true form of the name was *Eumenês* (Εὐμένης), and not
Eumênos (Εὔμηνος).

[8] Panofka, *Antiques du Musée Pourtalès-Gorgier*, Pl. XXVII.

types of Selinûs. It is at once obvious that both the Syracusan and Selinuntine types in question, must be referred
approximately to the same date. But Selinûs, as we
know, was destroyed in 409 b.c., and although this quadriga is the most advanced type found on the tetradrachms
of that city, there exist certain Selinuntine hêmidrachms, on
which the horses are seen in still higher action, and in one
case at least, the epigraphy assumes a slightly later form. It
is, therefore, probable, that the dies of the tetradrachms
referred to, though the latest of Selinûs, were engraved
some few years, at least, before 409 b.c. On the other
hand, from the early associations, in which their Syracusan
counterparts signed **EYΘ**. . . are found, it is difficult to
bring down the first issue of these latter later than about
420 b.c. Whether Syracuse or Selinûs can lay a prior
claim to the introduction of this scheme is another question. To myself the Syracusan version seems distinctly
earlier.

Dr. Weil, indeed, from the isolated character of this
design on the Syracusan coinage, was inclined to regard it
as due to the presence at Syracuse of some Selinuntine or
Akragantine [9] engraver, who had escaped from the destruction of his native city in 409 or 406 b.c. But the evidence
that this design is earlier than 409 b.c. must be taken to
diminish the plausibility of this suggestion. As a matter
of fact, the scheme is as isolated at Selinûs as it is at
Syracuse. And on the other hand, some newly-discovered
Siculo-Punic types, to which attention will be presently

---

[9] Dr. Weil, *loc. cit.* p. 9, sees Akragantine features in the
Skylla, which also occurs on a tetradrachm of that city (*B. M.
Cat.* p. 12, No. 61 ; Salinas, *Le Monete*, &c., Tav. 8, f. 3, 4)
and the fish, which is similar to one seen with the crab on
other Akragantine tetradrachms (*B. M. Cat.* No. 59 ; Salinas,
Tav. 8, f. 2) ; and further, in the arrangement of the chariot.

called, show that the Punic cities of Western Sicily copied the Syracusan and not the Selinuntine version of this reverse. That the design deviates from the usual Sicilian tradition is obvious. But it seems to me that another and more satisfactory explanation of its origin may be found. It stands, in fact, in a very close relation to a well-marked group of quadriga types that appear on some contemporary coins of Kyrênê. The even arrangement of the horses, the facing tendency of both horses and chariot, and the winged charioteers [10]—the three most characteristic points, both on the Syracusan and Selinuntine pieces—are all found on a fine series of Kyrênæan gold *staters* which, from the early character of their style and epigraphy, must have been struck about the same period as our Sicilian pieces, and which in fact mark the flourishing epoch of the civic history that ensued on the fall of the Battiadæ and the establishment of a Republican form of government at Kyrênê in 431 B.C.[11] But, whereas on the Sicilian dies the recurrence of such schemes is altogether isolated, in Kyrênê they are obviously at home, and we may even trace the genesis of one of the most important features of the design, the wings, namely, of the charioteer, which seem to have been suggested by the somewhat awkwardly flowing mantle of the driver on a slightly earlier *stater*.

It is possible that during the years that immediately preceded the Athenian siege, some Kyrênæan engraver was attracted by the opulence of Syracuse to settle in that

---

[10] The winged charioteer also appears on the coins of Akragas (where the same Kyrênæan influence may also be detected), and of Gela.

[11] Head, *Hist. Num.*, p. 729.

city ; but on the whole it seems more probable that the
introduction of these types, both at Syracuse and Selinûs,
was due to an active commercial intercourse between

Fig. 3.—Quadriga-Types on Kyrênæan Gold Staters.

Kyrênê and the ports of Southern Sicily and to the
direct influence of the brilliant gold coinage lately introduced in the great Doric plantation of the Libyan coast.[12]
The appearance of the two parallel designs about the same
time at Syracuse and Selinûs may in this case simply
indicate that engravers of both cities borrowed independently from a common source.

These Syracusan tetradrachms signed **EYO**, presenting
this Kyrênæan scheme of the quadriga, seem to have been

---

[12] The reciprocal influence of the Sicilian currency on that of
Kyrênê may, perhaps, be traced in the appearance at this time
of Kyrênæan gold pieces of $13\frac{1}{2}$ grains (cf. Head, *Hist. Num.* p.
729), answering to the weight of the silver litra. Gold litræ of
the same weight were issued at Gela—one in my possession
weighing $13\frac{1}{2}$ grains (see p. 99)—and the corresponding gold dilitron of the same city, weighing *c.* 27 grains, are better known.
Taking the proportional value of gold and silver as 15 to 1,
these coins must have severally represented three and six
drachms Æ. They thus range with the small Sicilian gold
pieces of 9 and 18 grains (cf. Head, *Coins of Syracuse*, p. 17),
which represent gold obols and diobols, and are the equivalent
in silver of didrachms and tetradrachms respectively ; so that,
by a combination of the litra and obol systems, we have a series
of small gold pieces, the silver value of which is two, three, four,
and six drachms.

specially selected for imitation by the Siculo-Punic die-
sinkers during the period of preparation which immediately
preceded the great Carthaginian invasion of 409 B.C. That
invasion, as was to be expected, left a deep impress on the
coinage of the Phœnician cities of Sicily, which is traceable
in several ways. During the late Transitional Period of
numismatic art, the continuous process of Hellenization
that was at work in the Phœnician and Elymian communi-
ties of the Western part of the Island, had left its mark on
the epigraphy of their coinage, insomuch that it is not
only at Segesta and Eryx that we find Greek inscriptions,
but at Panormos and even at Motya. But the great
reinforcement of Carthaginian authority in this Sicilian
region which followed on the invasion of 409, though it
did not interfere with the Hellenic taste of the inhabitants
so far as the artistic character of the coin-types was concerned, seems to have put an end for ever to the adoption
of Hellenic legends. The brilliant series of coins struck
shortly afterwards in the island by Carthage in her own
name for the use of her mercenaries did not by any means
extinguish the autonomous issues of the old Phœnician
cities of Sicily, but they were a speaking witness to the
new political situation. At Motya itself the coins now are
either wholly uninscribed or present the Semitic form of
the town name. The coins of the Panormitis are inscribed
with the still mysterious inscription "Ziz." But at the
same time the vast treasure taken from the plundered
Greek cities seems to have supplied fresh models to the
Siculo-Punic mints, and, it may be, even fresh engravers
from among the captive Greeks.

Some valuable and hitherto unattainable data for distinguishing these early Siculo-Punic types have been supplied
by the discovery of a recent hoard of silver coins

in Western Sicily, the bulk of which are now in the Museum at Palermo.[13] This find is of special import-ance to our present inquiry as containing a series of Siculo-Punic coins with heads copied from Kimôn's "medallions" (Types I. and II.), associated in several instances with quadriga types based on the Syracusan design by the engraver Euth . . . whose signature is here replaced in the same position in the exergue by the Phœnician inscription ꟼↄↄꟼ (Ziz), while the Skylla beside it is transformed into a sea-horse.

It is probable from the occurrence of the legend *Ziz* that these early silver types must be referred to the Panormitan mint.[14] Their attribution to this Phœnician city receives, moreover, an interesting corroboration from the fact that a copy of the same sea-horse on a smaller scale, and in an inferior style, was introduced into the exergue of the latest tetradrachms of the neighbouring Greek city of Himera by the engraver Mae . . . .[15] We thus obtain a valuable clue to the date of the earliest Siculo-Punic

---

[13] The coins have been described and illustrated by phototype plates, by Professor Salinas, in the *Notizie degli Scavi*, for 1888. (*Ripostiglio Siciliano di monete antiche di argento.*) In Appendix A. I have given some reasons for differing from Professor Salinas's chronological conclusions regarding this find.

[14] For the special connexion of the legend *Ziz* with Panormos, see De Saulcy, *Mém. de l'Acad. des Inscr. et B.L.* xv. 2, p. 46 *seqq.*, and *Rev. Num.*, 1844, p. 44-46. Imhoof Blumer, *Monnaies Grecques*, p. 26, inclines to the same view : " Si elle n'a pas une signification plus générale, qui n'aurait pas même besoin d'être géographique, elle doit être le nom Phénicien de Panormos, comme De Saulcy l'a vu le premier." In the *B. M. Cat.* they are placed under Panormos. Any identification of ꟼↄↄꟼ with the **IIB** on coins of Segesta and Eryx has pro-bably been set at rest for ever by Dr. Kinch's study on the latter epigraphic form.—*Die Sprache der sicilischen Elymer (Zeitschr. f. Num.* xvi. (1888), p. 187 *seqq.*)

[15] See p. 180 *seqq.* and Pl. X. 2.

K

coins of this group, which must, in this case, have been in existence by 409 B.C. when Himera was utterly destroyed. The official coins struck in Sicily in the name of Carthage, with which these autonomous Siculo-Punic pieces were associated in the find, are slightly later in style and, in all probability, date from the time of the second Carthaginian expedition of 406—405 B.C.[16]

It is probable that the presumably Panormitic pieces signed "*Ziz*" were struck from about 410 B.C. with a view to providing the expected Carthaginian ally with specie wherewith to pay his Campanian and other mercenaries. They thus supply a *terminus à quo* for the chronology of the obverse types which occur on them. These are of three kinds, all of which were represented in the West Sicilian find.

1. A female head, copied from an early head of Persephonê, by Eumenês. (*B. M. Cat.*, *Sicily*, p. 247, Nos. 8, 9; Salinas, *Ripostiglio Siciliano*, &c., Tav. xviii. 36, 37.)

2. A head copied from that of Arethusa in the net on Kimôn's earliest "medallion" (Type I.). (Salinas, *Ripostiglio*, &c., Tav. xviii. 34.) Cf. Plate I., Figs. 8, 9.

3. A head copied from that of Arethusa in the net on Kimôn's later "medallion" in high relief (Type II. A). (Salinas, *Ripostiglio*, Tav. xviii. 35.) Plate II., Fig. 7.

The importance of this conclusion in its bearing on the date of Kimôn's dekadrachms can hardly be overrated. From the identity of the reverse with which these various heads are coupled, and the similarity of their technique, it is obvious that all three of these Siculo-Punic types were struck within a few years of one another. Yet some of them had already, by 409 B.C., influenced the

---

[16] See p. 97.

character of the latest Himeræan coinage. It follows
that by that approximate date not only Kimôn's earliest
"medallions," with the low relief, had been already in
circulation, but his later and more advanced work, representing his earliest issue in high relief (Type II.), which
is copied by No. 3. And it follows as a corollary to this
that Kimôn's first dekadrachm issue, which is in a distinctly less advanced style than those in high relief, must
have been struck some years at least before the issue of
these Siculo-Punic types which belong to what may be
called the great Carthaginian re-coinage of 410 and the
immediately ensuing years.

The fact, moreover, that in two cases we find the
imitation of Kimôn's work associated with copies of the
reverse type by Euth . . . must in itself be considered
a strong indication that Kimôn's early "medallions"
go back, at least, to the borders of the period when
Euth . . . engraved his dies. But the Kyrênæan design of this latter artist belongs, as already shown, to the
period immediately preceding the Athenian siege, and
we are thus induced by more than one line of reasoning
to throw back Kimôn's first dekadrachm issue to a date
somewhat nearer 415 than 410 B.C.

The West Sicilian hoard to which reference has already
been made, and which, from the place where it was discovered, it may be convenient to give the name of the
"Contessa Find," has supplied in addition to the above-
mentioned Panormitic types one or two examples of
Motyan tetradrachms also copied on their obverse sides
from Kimôn's "medallion" types and struck no doubt on
the same occasion as the coins signed *Ziz*. These are :—

1. *Obv.*—Female head to r., with hair in net, and with earring of a single drop, in high relief and fine style,

copied from the head of Arethusa in the net on Kimôn's later dekadrachms (Type II.). Insc. (*Motua*) 𐤌𐤈𐤅𐤀.

Rev.—Crab.

(Salinas, *Ripostiglio*, &c., Tav. xviii. 17. One example found.) [Pl. II. fig. 5.]

2. *Obv.*—Female head to l., with hair in net and earring with bar and three pendants, copied from Kimôn's later dekadrachm, but in an inferior and obviously later style.

(Salinas, *Ripostiglio*, &c., Tav. xviii. 18. Three examples found.) [Pl. II. fig. 6.]

The evidence brought to light by this find of the influence exercised by Kimôn's works on the Motyan engravers fits on to the witness already supplied by some smaller silver and bronze pieces of this Phœnician city. A didrachm of Motya of which examples from two dies exist (Pl. III. figs. 11, 12),[17] presents the facing head of a Nymph surrounded by dolphins, obviously copied from the facing head of Arethusa, with Kimôn's signature, on the well-known Syracusan tetradrachm, and this didrachm in its turn was reproduced on a series of silver obols[18] (Pl. III. fig. 10) and small bronze pieces[19] (Pl. III., fig. 8)

---

[17] For Pl. III., fig. 12, see *B. M. Cat., Sicily*, p. 244, No. 8; Weil, *Künstlerinschriften*, &c., p. 29. Pl. III., fig. 11, is from the Paris Cabinet.

[18] *B. M. Cat.. Sicily*, p. 244, No. 9.

[19] In the *B. M. Cat.* (p. 245) these small bronze pieces appear as "Motya?" I have, however, myself obtained several on the actual site of Motya, the small island of St. Pantaleo, between Trapani and Marsala; and as these small coins were for local circulation only, this evidence may be regarded as conclusive. On one of these small bronze coins the face and head of the Nymph seems to be coupled on the other side, not as usual with a youthful male head, but with a small copy of the profile head of Arethusa in the net (*B. M. Cat., Motya*, 20, described as a "young male head"). This head, in very high relief, is probably taken from one of the gold hundred-litra pieces engraved by Kimôn or Evænetos, the young male head which accompanies

issued by the Motyan mint during the last period of the civic existence.

The existence of a whole series of Motyan coins copied from prototypes by Kimôn in his more advanced style is itself a valuable chronological landmark, since Motya itself was utterly overthrown by Dionysios in 397 B.C. The discovery in the Contessa Hoard of two varieties of Motyan coins imitated from Kimôn's dekadrachm of high relief (Type II.), one of which is distinctly posterior in style to the other, further enables us to throw back the latest possible date of the first issue of Kimôn's later "medallions" some years, at least, before 400 B.C., beyond which year, as I have endeavoured to show in Appendix A, it is impossible to bring down the deposit of this West Sicilian find. In this find, besides the Panormitic and Motyan imitations, there was one somewhat used original example of Kimôn's later " medallion " (Type II.).[20]

A still more remarkable contribution to the chronology of Kimôn's medallions is supplied by his beautiful tetradrachm type representing the three-quarters facing Arethusa (Pl. III. figs. 4, 5), which amongst all the dies executed by this artist, must ever be regarded as his masterpiece. But the face represented so closely corresponds with the profile portrait on Kimôn's later dekadrachm with the high relief (Type III.), that it is impossible to suppose that more than a few years could have intervened between the engraving of their respective dies. And in the case of Kimôn's facing head of Arethusa

other Motyan bronze types being in the same way derived from the head of the River God on the contemporary gold fifty-litra pieces of Syracuse. It thus appears that both these classes of Syracusan gold coins were current several years before the fall of Motya.

[20] Salinas, *Ripostiglio*, &c., Tav. xvii. 21.

we have more than one trustworthy guide to the date of its first issue.

The imitation of this noble type on a series of Motyan coins, is itself an indication that it had been in existence several years at least before 397 B.C., the date of the destruction of that Phœnician city by Dionysios. Its influence seems further traceable in the facing head of Kamarina on a drachm of that city (Pl. III., fig. 9), and another of the River-God Amenanos by Choiriôn at Katanê (Pl. III., fig. 6). But a still more important piece of evidence is supplied by the small bronze coin of Himera[21] of which a reproduction is given in fig. 4.

Fig. 4.—Copy of Kimôn's Arethusa on Bronze Coin of Himera.

There can be no doubt that the three-quarters facing head of the Nymph on this Himeræan *hémilitron* is directly and very literally copied from Kimôn's head of Arethusa. But Himera itself was utterly wiped out by the Carthaginians at the close of 409 B.C., and it is evident that, late as this type must be placed in the Himeræan series, the original design from which it was copied cannot therefore be brought down later than that year. We may even infer that this Himeræan copy was called forth under the immediate influences of the impression created by the first appearance of Kimôn's masterpiece, and ascribe the issue of the Syracusan original, with some confidence, to

---

[21] *B. M. Cat. Himera*, No. 55 ; *rev.* IME, crayfish l., above, • • • • • • = 6 οὐγκίαι. It was therefore a *hémilitron*.

the year 409. Earlier than this it can hardly be; the quadriga schemes indeed on the two reverses with which it is coupled bear the closest resemblance to those which mark the latest tetradrachm issue of Gela struck during the years that immediately preceded its destruction in 405.[22] The ear of barley, moreover, on the exergue, which accompanies Kimôn's reverses, reappears in the same position as the Gelan coins.[23]

The date of Kimôn's beautiful tetradrachm with the facing head of Arethusa thus approximately established, affords, as already observed, a sure guide to the approximate chronology of Kimôn's later " medallions," with the head in profile of the same Nymph. In spite of the difference in the point of view from which the two faces are taken, their correspondence in expression and physiognomy is most striking, though the slightly more advanced style of the dekadrachm (Type III.) may incline us to bring down its date of issue a few years later.

The considerable difference in style between Kimôn's earlier type of Arethusa on his dekadrachm of lower relief and that of his later issues, does not necessarily imply any great discrepancy of date. As a matter of fact, both classes are accompanied by the same reverse type, nor had the dies of the reverse at all deteriorated at the time when Kimôn's later " medallions" were first struck. The difference in style is largely to be attributed to other causes. In the case of his original design for the head of Arethusa, Kimôn, as will be shown more fully in the course of this paper, himself of non-Syracusan extraction, was evidently bound down by the traditions of the Syra-

[22] B. M. Cat. Nos. 58, 59.
[23] Pertinent parallels from the same period of years may also be cited from Kamarina and other cities.

cusan mint, and contented himself with improving and elaborating with excessive richness of detail a pre-existing model. By the time that he executed his bolder designs of the tutelary Nymph, he may well have acquired a more assured position in his new home, and could give freer vent to the promptings of his own genius and to the independent art-traditions that he had brought with him.

What those traditions were and whence he brought them, is best shown by the evidence of his masterpiece, the facing head of Arethusa. Before, however, entering on this part of our subject, it may be well to consider this noble work in its relation to contemporary Sicilian attempts at a perspective rendering of the human face, and to glance at the influence of Kimôn's artistic triumph on the Hellenic world and its borderlands.

The fact that a perspective rendering of the three-quarters face should have appeared at Syracuse as early as 409 B.C., need not in itself surprise us. The comparison which Kimôn's masterpiece most naturally calls up is the three-quarters facing head of Pallas in the triple-crested helmet by the contemporary Syracusan artist Eukleidas. From the character of the reverse with which it is accompanied, and which bears a marked resemblance to those executed by Evarchidas, in honour, it has been suggested, of a naval victory gained over the Athenians,[24] there seem

---

[24] See Salinas (*Ripostiglio Siciliano*, &c., p. 15—18 and Tav. xxiii. 25) and *Num. Chron.* (1890, p. 301 *seqq.*, and Pl. XVIII., 6, 7), where I have accepted Prof. Salinas's suggestion that the *aplustre* held by Nikê refers to a naval victory over the Athenians. From the somewhat early character of the obverse heads by Phrygillos, which seem to date from the period before the Athenian siege, it is preferable, however, to suppose that the trophy refers to the earlier victory of the winter of 414-413, rather than that of September, 413.

to me to be good reasons for referring this famous design
to a date at least as early as Kimôn's head of Arethusa,
indeed an example of Eukleidas' tetradrachm occurred
in the famous Naxos hoard buried about 410 B.C.[25] It
is, however, to be observed that though in this case the
artist was greatly aided by the helmet in overcoming the
difficulties of a facing portraiture, his design fails to convey that sense of freedom and of mastery over technical
difficulties that looks forth from Kimôn's Arethusa. The
same is true of the facing head of the young River-God

Fig. 5.—Triobol of Selinûs.

Hipparis, by Evænetos, on a didrachm of Kamarina that
also belongs to this period.[26]

Dr. Weil has already called attention to the fact that
the three-quarters head of Hêraklês which appears on a
hêmidrachm of Selinûs must have been engraved before
the date of the overthrow of that city, and I am now
able to reproduce in Fig. 5 another Selinuntine silver
piece of the same denomination,[27] in which the head of

---

[25] See Appendix B. For Eukleidas' tetradrachm see *B. M.
Cat.*, 198, 199; Weil, *Künstlerinschriften*, Taf. iii. 7.

[26] *B. M. Cat.* No. 16; Weil, *Künstlerinschriften*, &c., Taf.
ii. 6. That this is by no means one of the latest types of
Kamarina is shown by the fact that the reverse design of the
nymph riding over the waves of her lake, which is also evidently
from Evænetos's hand, was copied on more than one die by the
local (and inferior) engraver, Exakestidas.

[27] The weight of this coin is 28 grs.: it is therefore a triobol.
A caricature apparently intended to represent this coin was
published by Castelli (Tav. lxvi. 2), but since his time the
type has been lost sight of.

L

the youthful God appears almost full-facing, and with the
mane of the lion's scalp, with which he is coifed, waving
behind him in every direction, in a manner suggestive of
Arethusa's tresses on Kimôn's die. Yet this coin also
must have been issued by 409 B.C.

The fact that these other Sicilian examples are not so
advanced in their treatment of perspective as the masterpiece of the Syracusan engraver, does not then prove any
real discrepancy of date. That Kimôn, in his facing head
of Arethusa, had achieved something that went beyond
anything that had been hitherto accomplished in this
branch of engraving, is shown by the great impression it
made on his contemporaries, and that not only in Sicily
itself, at Himera, or at Phœnician but Hellenized Motya,
but in the Mother-Country of Greêce and even in the
Asiatic borderlands of Greek and Oriental. And the early
date of the imitations of Kimôn's design thus called into
being is specially noteworthy. Already, by the end of
the Fifth and the first years of the Fourth Century B.C. it
had been taken as the model for the beautiful series of
Nymphs' heads, which from this time forth for the better
part of a century adorn the coinage of the Thessalian
Larissa[28] (Pl. III. 13—15), and soon after 400 B.C. it had
been adopted as the obverse design for their Staters by
the Satraps of the Æolid and Cilicia (Pl. III. fig. 16).[29]

---

[28] B. M. Cat. Thessaly, &c., Pl. V. 14, VI. 1—12. I quite
agree with Weil's verdict, op. cit. p. 81, that the earliest Laris-
san designs of this head are copied from Kimôn's "Mit allem
Detail in der Behandlung der Locken." Gardner, Types of
Greek Coins, p. 154, does not go beyond the resemblance. From
Larissa the type seems to have spread to Gomphi (B. M. Cat.,
Pl. III. 2—4).

[29] Duc de Luynes, Numismatique des Satrapies (1846, p. 6),
and cf. J. P. Six, Le Satrape Mazaïos (Num. Chron. 1884, p.

But the facing head of Arethusa on the Syracusan coin itself had a prototype. Another comparison remains, which not only throws a light on the sources from which Kimôn himself drew, but has a suggestive bearing on his own early history. There can, I venture to think, be little doubt that this beautiful design was itself in its essential lineaments derived from the beautiful three-quarters facing head of a Nymph—we may call her Parthenopê—which makes its appearance in the immediately preceding period on some didrachms of Neapolis.[30] (Pl. III., figs. 1, 2). The arrangement of the locks, the *ampyx* and its border, the character of the eyes, the dimples about the lips, the whole expression of countenance, present such remarkable points of agreement, that it is even difficult not to believe that both are by the same hand, and that Kimôn's initials may some day be detected on the band of the Neapolitan coins. The style of the engraving is also very similar to the finely incised lines of the hair, and recalls the use of the diamond point on gems of the same period. The greater simplicity of the Neapolitan design shows, however, that it is the original and not the copy. Its comparatively early date is, moreover, indicated by the style of the reverse and the *boustrophêdon* epigraphy—the civic legend appearing in the transitional

124 *seqq.*, Pl. VI. 6, 8). M. Six assigns the earliest of these coins to the approximate date 394—387 B.C. Then follow others struck by Pharnabazos and Tarkamos, 387—373. The Duc de Luynes' attribution of a coin of this type to Mania, wife of Zenis, Satrap of Æolis (*op. cit.*, p. 48; *Suppl.*, Pl. VI. 2), who was strangled in 399 B.C., is untenable. M. Babelon has succeeded in tracing the original referred to in the *Cabinet des Médailles*, and the coin engraved turns out to be a misinterpreted bronze piece of Dardanos of later date with a three-quarters facing head of Apollo.

[30] *B. M. Cat., Italy*, p. 94, No. 11.

form **NEOΠOVI** **ꙅHT**, and it fits on to still earlier versions of the same head in which the legend takes the form **NEOΠOVI**[31] **ꙅHT** and **NEOΠOVI**[32] **ꙅꙅT** A companion-piece will be found in the beautiful Phistelian didrachm (Pl. III., fig. 3). The earliest of these coins must be referred to the years immediately succeeding the fall of Kymê, which took place in 423 B.C., and the immediate prototype of Kimôn's Arethusa is probably itself as early as 415.

The coincidences of style, design, and technique that reveal themselves between Kimôn's three-quarters facing head of Arethusa and the slightly earlier head on the Neapolitan coin do not by any means stand alone. The profile head of Arethusa in the net on Kimôn's later "medallions," as upon his fine tetradrachm, present both in their style and characteristic features a suggestive resemblance to the profile heads of Parthenopê and her sisters that about the same time make their appearance on some of the finest coins of Neapolis, Hyrina, and Nola. Examining such Campanian coin-types as those figured, Pl. II. 9—11, we notice the same bold relief, the recurrence of certain details in the ornament, to which attention will be more fully called, and a certain similarity in the manner of treating the hair, but above all we are struck by the same indefinable haughtiness of expression which forms such a marked characteristic of Kimôn's beautiful heads of Arethusa, and which in her case so fittingly bespeaks the double nature of her mythic being—half Nymph, half Artemis.

These Campanian affinities have an additional value when taken in connection with the range of Kimôn's

---

[31] Garrucci, *Le Monete*, &c., Tav. lxxxiv. 24.
[32] *Op. cit.*, Tav. lxxxiv. 23.

known activity in Sicily itself, and with the high probability suggested by a recently discovered type that he
himself was of Chalkidian stock. In a preceding communication[33] I have already endeavoured to show that
about the middle of the Fifth Century B.C. an earlier
Kimôn left his signature on a fine tetradrachm of Himera,
and have suggested that in this earlier artist we may
venture to recognise the grandfather of the Kimôn who
toward the close of the same century worked for the
Syracusan mint. I further showed[34] that this later Kimôn
executed more than one tetradrachm die for Messana, the
Chalkidian mother-city of Himera, at a date slightly
anterior to his first employment for the Syracusan coinage.
As a matter of fact, while there is evidence of collabora-
tion and interconnexion between the other contemporary
engravers of the Syracusan dies, the signature of Eumenês
being coupled on the same piece with that of one or other
of his apparent pupils, Evænetos and Eukleidas, and that
of Phrygillos with Evarchidas,—the reverses of Euth. . .
forming a link between the two,—Kimôn stands by himself, and except on a single drachm with IM on the observe
his name is not associated with that of any other die-
sinker.

That this engraver, who appears thus isolated in the
Syracusan series, who on the dies of Syracuse introduces
a Neapolitan type and a Campanian style, and who was,
as we have seen, doubly connected with Chalkidian cities
of the East and North Sicilian shores, had himself originally received his artistic training in one or other of the
sister colonies on the opposite Tyrrhenian coast will

---

[33] " Some New Artists' Signatures on Sicilian Coins," *Num.
Chron.*, 1890, p. 285 *seqq.* (P. 173 *seqq.* of this volume.)
[34] *Op. cit.*, p. 298 *seqq.* (P. 186 *seqq.* of this volume.)

hardly be thought an improbable conclusion. That he worked at least for one Italian mint appears certain from the occurrence of his signature on a silver stater of Metapontion,[35] presenting a female head, perhaps of Nikê, in style somewhat later than a head of the same general character on one of the latest coins of Kymê. The special connexion of Kimôn with the Chalkidian cities of Campania is, however, brought out, as already noticed, by an ornamental feature which, though at first sight it may appear trivial, will be found to afford a very tangible clue both to the extraction of the artist and the date of his dies. The forms of earring, namely, with which Kimôn's heads of Arethusa are adorned, are foreign to Syracusan and indeed to Sicilian [36] fashions, but on the other hand are closely akin to a type that is specially characteristic of the contemporary dies of Neapolis and her sister cities.

On the earliest coins of Syracuse on which this ornament appears, from the beginning of the Fifth Century onwards, it takes the form of a ring somewhat boat-shaped below and provided with an appendage that sometimes consists of a pyramid of beads or of one larger and two smaller globules, perhaps an outgrowth of the Homeric ἕρματα τρίγληνα μορόεντα.[37] About the middle of the Fifth Century this

---

[35] Garrucci, *Le Monete dell' Italia antica*, Tav. ciii., Fig. 16 and p. 187. In Garrucci's own collection. The inscription, according to Garrucci, is "KIMΩN"; so far as the engraving is concerned, the Ω might be an incomplete O. Both text and engravings of Garrucci's book must, unfortunately, be used with caution.

[36] With the partial exception of the Segestan tetradrachm referred to above as in many ways a parallel piece to Kimôn's early dekadrachms.

[37] See Helbig, *Das Homerische Epos*, p. 271 *seqq.*, and compare especially Figs. 97, 98, p. 274, with the Syracusan example in Head, *Coins of Syracuse*, Pl. II., Fig. 10, &c.

fashion gives way to an earring in the form of a coiled ring (*helix*) which is still universally adopted by Eumenês, Sôsiôn, Eukleidas, and on the earlier work of Evænetos. Of the earlier engravers, Phrygillos alone occasionally discards it for a whorl-shell, a form of earring which also occurs in the ear of Aphroditê on an archaic terra-cotta relief found on the site of Gela,[38] as well as in that of Persephonê Sôsipolis on the gold litras of that city. In the Fourth Century, on the other hand, we find the coiled ring and all other forms of earring abandoned in favour of the type exhibiting a bar and three pendants. The earliest coins on which this latter form makes its appearance are apparently the dekadrachm by the New Artist and the gold hundred-litra pieces of both Kimôn and Evænetos. It was from the first adopted by Evænetos for his "medallions," and henceforth became of universal use on the Syracusan dies.

On the other hand, the forms which occur on Kimôn's dekadrachms stand apart from those employed by all other

Pendants: A. Egyptian ; B. Etruscan ; C. Phœnician. Earrings: D. Kimôn's Medallions ; E. Campanian.
Fig. 6.—Lotos Ornament and Earrings.

Syracusan engravers. His earlier head of Arethusa is seen adorned with a very beautiful floral form of earring, consisting of a lotos flower with three drops (Fig. 6, D).

---

[38] Now in the Ashmolean Museum at Oxford.

The decorative design is itself of Egyptian origin[39] and finds close parallels in Phœnician,[40] Cypriote,[41] and Etruscan[42] pendants; it is interesting, however, to note that as a Greek fashion it seems to have been specially rife among the Campanian cities. From about 420 B.C. onwards a form closely allied to that introduced at Syracuse by Kimôn was in vogue at Neapolis, Hyrina, and Nola (Fig. 6, E), and it was only late in the Fourth Century that among the Campanian Greeks this floral type gave way to the bar and triple pendant. Upon Sicilian coins I am only aware of a single instance beside this early dekadrachm of Kimôn in which this floral form is introduced; and that in a very modified form. A somewhat analogous type, namely, is found on the beautiful head of the Nymph Segesta upon the tetradrachm of that city,[43] which has already been cited as standing in much the same typological relation to the Arethusa head of Evænetos' early manner as the head upon Kimôn's *pentêkontalitron*. On the dekadrachms in Kimôn's more advanced style and the tetradrachms that accompanied them, a simpler form of earring, consisting of a single drop, makes its appearance.

This form is also strange to the Syracusan dies, but like the last, it finds abundant parallels on the Italian side. It is found at Kymê before 423 B.C. and slightly later at Neapolis. It seems, moreover, to have been specially fashionable at Metapontion, where it appears on the heads

---

[39] Cf. Perrot et Chipiez, *Égypte*, p. 834, fig. 569, on bands of collar imitating pendants (xxii. Dyn.). (Fig. 6, A.)

[40] Perrot et Chipiez, *Phénicie*, p. 827, fig. 588. (Fig. 6, C.)

[41] Cesnola, *Cyprus*, Pl. XXIII. (Fig. 6, B.)

[42] *Museum Gregorianum*, T. lxxx. 4. (Fig. 6, B.)

[43] Pl. I., 4. It is well shown in the engraving in Salinas' *Sul tipo de' tetradrammi di Segesta* (Florence, 1871), Tav. I. f. 2.

of Hygieia and Homonoia of Late Transitional style, and it continues during the Period of Perfect Art, gradually giving place, however, to more ornamental forms, and finally to the bar and triple pendant. That these forms of earring introduced by Kimón did not hit Sicilian taste[44] seems clear both from their non-acceptance by his successors at Syracuse itself, and by the fact that in the later of the Motyan imitations of his "medallion" head they are discarded in favour of the new fashion. On some of the Panormitic pieces, struck about 410 B.C., a variety of the triple pendant already appears, and it looks as if this form of the ornament had reached Syracuse under Carthaginian influence a few years later.

Recapitulating the conclusions arrived at on various grounds with regard to the date of Kimón's "medallion" types, we arrive at the following results. The earliest of these (Type I.), representing the head of Arethusa in low relief (Pl. I., fig. 5), belongs to the years immediately succeeding 415 B.C., and in all probability, as I hope to show in a succeeding section, the date of its issue corresponds with the institution of the New Games in honour of the Athenian overthrow of 413 B.C.

Closely following this, but in higher relief, is the type which in my account of the Santa Maria hoard has been described as Type II. (Pl. II., fig. 1). It has not the full human individuality of expression that characterises Kimón's more developed head of Arethusa as she appears, facing on the tetradrachm and in profile on his latest dekadrachm type. With this "medallion" issue corresponds the exquisite tetradrachm (Pl. II., fig. 2)

[44] It is to be observed that on Kimón's gold hundred-litra pieces the bar-earring with the triple pendant is used. In this case he seems to have simply imitated Evænetos' model.

with the profile head of the Nymph in high relief, and accompanied by a slightly earlier reverse scheme than those which appear on the coins with the facing head. The earliest of Kimôn's gold hundred-litra pieces (Pl. II. 3, 4) also reproduce the same facial type. Of Kimôn's later "medallions," it seems to be Type II., only, that was imitated on the coins of Panormos and Motya, belonging, as has been already pointed out, to the Phœnician re-coinage about the time of the First Carthaginian expedi-tion. It is probable, therefore, that this "medallion" type was issued as early as 410 B.C.

Next come the dekadrachms described as Type III. (Pl. II., fig. 8), exhibiting a portraiture of Arethusa, which is simply the profile rendering of the same queenly countenance that looks forth from his masterpiece—the tetradrachm with the facing head and the inscription ΑΡΕΘΟΣΑ, struck, as has been shown above, about 409 B.C. These coins represent the supreme develop-ment of Kimôn's style, and the individuality of features and expression clearly indicate that they are both of them taken from the same living model, whose beautiful but distinctly haughty face haunts all Kimôn's later pre-sentations of the tutelary Nymph, in much the same manner as the idealised heads of Andrea's wife or Raffaelle's mistress look forth from their Madonnas.

The very intimate relation existing between the portrait on this "medallion" and the facing head on the tetra-drachm forbids us to bring down the date of the earliest example much below the year 409. On the other hand, its somewhat later style and the fact that this type was not, like the other two, imitated by the Siculo-Punic copy-ists of Kimôn's "medallions," who seem to have executed their dies during the years immediately succeeding 410

B.C., may incline us to bring it down as late as the beginning of the Dionysian Tyranny and approximately to the year 406. There is, however, more than one variety of this type, and as some of these are executed in a distinctly inferior style, we are justified in supposing that they belong to a somewhat later date.

The earliest and most exquisite example of the medallions in Kimôn's fully developed style is that engraved on Pl. II. fig. 8, and may be described as Type III. A.[45] It is much rarer than the coarser variety. The exquisite finish shown in the engraving of this head rivals that of Kimôn's earliest work, and in one small but beautiful detail it stands alone amongst portraits of this artist. This is the indication of the upper eyelashes, a minute touch frequent on heads of the late Transitional Period at Syracuse, and still repeated by the earlier master, Eumenês, but which on the later signed coins is no longer seen. Parallelism of style and expression shows that Kimôn's later gold staters (Pl. II., fig. 9) belong to the same Period as this "medallion" type.

What, however, may be called the rank and file of Kimôn's later "medallions," though in other respects copied from this model, show a distinct falling off in their execution. These coins, of which more than one small variety exists, may be grouped together as Type III. B, and they represent the most abundant of Kimôn's dekadrachm issues. It is possible that they were first issued two or three years later than Type III. A. From

---

[45] *B. M. Cat., Syracuse*, No. 201 ; Head, *Coins of Syracuse*, Pl. IV. 7. The band above the forehead on this coin bears no inscription. Examples exist in the British Museum and the Cabinet des Médailles (Luynes Collection).

the fact, however, that, though the commonest of Kimôn's types, they are still rare by comparison with those of the rival artist, and from the strict adherence to a single model, it is not probable that their latest dies were executed much beyond the close of the Fifth Century.

PART V

THE ARTISTIC CAREER OF EVÆNETOS AND THE INFLUENCE OF HIS "MEDALLION"-TYPE ON GREEK, PHŒNICIAN AND CELT.

THE earliest numismatic record of Evænetos on the Syracusan dies or elsewhere is to be found on the remarkable tetradrachm (Pl. I. 3),[1] already referred to as the prototype of Kimôn's earliest "medallion," which was imitated in a more advanced style at Himera before 408 B.C., and, as will be shown more fully in the course of this section, at Segesta by about 415.[2]

The head on this coin, struck in all probability before 420 B.C.—perhaps as early as 425—is a masterpiece for the date at which it was engraved. Nothing can surpass the gemlike minuteness with which every detail, both of the obverse and reverse designs, is here elaborated. The ingenuity displayed is marvellous. To indicate apparently that the portrait is intended for Arethusa, the Nymph of the fountain by the waves, a dolphin, hardly visible to

---

[1] *B. M. Cat.*, *Sicily*, No. 188 ; Weil, *Künstlerinschriften*, &c., Taf. ii. 1, and p. 10. Von Sallet, *Künstlerinschriften*, &c., p. 17 ; Raoul Rochette, *Lettre, &c., sur les Graveurs*, Pl. II. 6, and p. 25, &c.

[2] Its early date is also indicated by the frequent association of the reverse with obverse types of the earlier master Eumenês. (Cf. *B. M. Cat.*, *Sicily*, p. 166, Nos. 148—150.)

ordinary eyes, is engraved on the front band of the sphendonê, leaping over the crested billows, just as on the parallel example of the same head executed by the contemporary and fellow-worker Eukleidas, a swan appears in a like position. The signature on the obverse is hidden in a most unexpected quarter. By a sportive device the larger dolphin, swimming in front of the Nymph's lips, turns over and reveals upon its belly in microscopic characters the first four letters of the artist's name. Upon the reverse Nikê, while flying forward to crown the charioteer, holds aloft a suspended tablet, bearing the full signature of the die-sinker in the early genitival form, **EYAINETO**. The bearded charioteer has still an archaic aspect, but the scheme of the horses, which are themselves exquisitely modelled, is altogether modern in the sensational incident of the chariot-race that it so graphically depicts. The rein of the farthest horse is broken, and has entangled itself round his foreleg and that of the horse beside him,[3] so that a worse catastrophe seems imminent.

On other tetradrachms associated with heads either by Eumenês or Eukleidas, there is seen a reverse of a slightly later style containing the signature of Evænetos, in the same full-length form, in microscopic letters on the exergual line beneath the chariot.[4] On this later reverse, in which the same episode of the tangled and trailing rein occurs, the sensation is heightened by the insertion of a broken chariot-wheel into the exergual space. A similar reverse, but with a head like that of the

---

[3] This entanglement of the rein, which is clearly visible on a fine specimen of this coin in my own collection, seems hitherto to have escaped observation.

[4] *B. M. Cat., Sicily*, p. 173, No. 190.

first-mentioned tetradrachm,[5] from the hand of Evænetos, also occurs on a very beautiful hêmidrachm [6] (Pl. VII. Fig. 8).

For the date at which they were engraved these tetradrachms of Evænetos are without a rival, and should by themselves be sufficient to give pause to those critics who would seek the full bloom of sensationalism on the Sicilian coin-types within the limits of the Dionysian epoch.

Compared with Evænetos' later dies, and notably his "medallions," the head of Arethusa, as it appears on his early tetradrachms and kindred hêmidrachms, has been justly described by Von Sallet as executed in his "early manner." They were the works, he considers, of Evænetos' youth, the dekadrachms of his mature age, and the two designs "stand to one another, if it is allowable to compare small things with great, as the *Spozalizio* to the *Madonna di San Sisto*. The gracefulness and chasteness of the small individual figures on the tetradrachms, the careful execution of the ornamentation and embroidery, all this greatly recalls the youthful works of Raffaelle and other Italian painters in contrast to their masterpieces, which—as in the case of dekadrachms—treat the details in a freer and less minute fashion." [7]

The general justice of this criticism no one can doubt. Between the execution by this artist of his early tetradrachm dies and those of his "medallions" there must have elapsed a considerable period of years.[8] At Syracuse, indeed, Evænetos is found again, apparently, as

---

[5] *B. M. Cat.*, Nos. 151 and 190 ; Head, *Coins of Syracuse*, iv. 4 ; Weil, *op. cit.*, Tav. iii. 6.

[6] Head, *op. cit.*, Pl. III. 16.

[7] Von Sallet, *Künstlerinschriften auf griechischen Münzen*, p. 20.

[8] Von Sallet, *loc. cit.*, allows an interval of two or three decennia between the two styles.

we shall see, in the years succeeding the defeat of the Athenians, executing the dies of the new gold hundred-and fifty-litra pieces. But the execution of these fits on to his later style, as seen upon his earliest silver deka-drachms, and from the evidence at our disposal we must conclude that there had intervened a period, partly covered by the Athenian siege, during which, for some unexplained reason, his connexion with the Syracusan mint had temporarily ceased.

This gap is, in all probability, partly covered by his activity at Katanê, where he produced two types, the tetra-drachms (Pl. VII. Fig. 9, a and b) with the head of Apollo and the Delphic fillet,[9] and the drachms (Pl. VII. Fig. 10) with the head of the young river-god Amenanos,[10] which from a certain severity in their design must still be in-cluded amongst the works executed in his " early manner," though they are apparently slightly later than the Syra-cusan tetradrachm referred to. On the reverse of the former of these coins, on which the charioteer is seen in the act of rounding the goal, Nikê appears above holding out to him a tablet bearing the first letters of the name of the engraver, a device which brings this coin into a very close relation with Evænetos' early Syracusan works. The chariot with the broken wheel below, on the drachms exhibiting the head of Amenanos, is in fact the companion piece to those on Evænetos' early Syracusan tetradrachms and hêmidrachms.

To this period of Evænetos' activity also unquestionably belongs the beautiful didrachm of Kamarina (Pl. VII. Fig.

---

[9] B. M. Cat., Sicily, p. 48, No. 35 ; Weil, op. cit., Taf ii. 4, 4 a ; Raoul Rochette, op. cit., Pl. I. 8.

[10] B. M. Cat., p. 48, Nos. 36—39 ; Weil, op. cit., Taf. ii. 5 ; Raoul Rochette, op. cit., Pl. I. 9.

11), with the facing head of the **river-god** Hipparis,[11] the reverse design of which with the **local Nymph** upon her swan, sailing over the waters of her lake, was copied in the succeeding years on a series of dies by the local engraver Exakestidas. The swan above the waves, accompanied by the same freshwater fish that is seen beneath on the didrachm of Evænetos, occurs by itself on contemporary Kamarinæan obols of the same period, the obverse of which displays a **female head** in a starred sphendonê, recalling that artist's early Syracusan design.

Besides the evidence of Evænetos' activity during this interval at Katanê and Kamarina, there is, I venture to think, a strong piece of circumstantial evidence connecting this artist about the same date with the Segestan mint. The fine head of the Nymph Segesta that appears on a tetradrachm of that Elymian city (Pl. I. Fig. 4),[12] recalls, not only in its general expression, but in the minutest details, the Arethusa of Evænetos' early Syracusan dies. The formation of the eye, and slight—almost imperceptible—incurving at the spring of the nose, the delicate folds of the neck, are reproduced in such a way as to make us conscious of very similar touch, and the arrangement of the hair, though it shows a greater development, as if to give promise of the curling tresses of Evænetos' Korê, is substantially the same. On the other hand there are certain **features** in the design, such as the indication of the upper eyelashes and the laced fringe of the sphendonê, that are taken, not from Evænetos' early head of Arethusa, but from the head as it appears on a die

---

[11] *B. M. Cat.*, *Kamarina*, No. 16.
[12] *B. M. Cat.*, No. 32; Salinas, *Sul tipo de' tetradrammi di Segesta*, Tav. 1. 2. The obverse legend is ϞΕΛΕϞΤΑΧΙΑ; the reverse ϞΕΓΕϞΤΑΙΩΝ.

N

of the earlier artist Eumenês, from which he himself copied.[13]

This variation in the design—still according with the artistic tradition of Evænetos—may be taken as a strong indication that this beautiful head of Segesta must be referred, if not to Evænetos himself, at least to some Syracusan pupil of that engraver.

One feature alone—the earring—is new. It belongs to a later fashion, and is interesting as presenting a form intermediate between the lotus-flower pattern and the simple triple pendant of Evænetos' later coins.[14] Whether the reverse type of this coin, representing the youthful river-god Krimisos pausing in the chase, be from the same hand as the head of the Nymph Segesta, it would be more difficult to determine, but it is in any case a work of which Evænetos himself might have been proud.

And with regard to the date of this Segestan coin we have some very clear indications both numismatic and historical. It belongs to a small and exceedingly rare class of coins of this denomination, presenting transitional traits both in their epigraphy and art, which unquestionably owed their origin to the exhaustive and by no means scrupulous efforts of the Segestans to secure and maintain the active co-operation of the Athenians, in their struggle against the combined Selinuntines and Syracusans, by imposing on their old allies with an exaggerated show of their opulence and splendour. Readers of Thucydides will be familiar with the story of how the "Egestæans" took in the Athenian envoys by borrowing plate from other cities as well as their own Treasury and passing it on

---

[13] *B. M. Cat., Sicily*, p. 166, No. 152 ; Weil, *op. cit.*, Taf. l. 7.
[14] See p. 79.

from one entertainer to another, or how they paraded to
them their offerings in the temple of Eryx, which, though
only of silver, seem from the impression they produced to
have been coated with the more precious metal.[15] That
the citizens now for the first time minted a fine tetradrachm coinage executed by the first artists of the day
in place of the somewhat rude didrachm issues with which
they had hitherto contented themselves, is all of a piece
with this parade of borrowed plate and silver-gilt goblets.
There is every reason then for confining this Segestan
show-coinage to the period between the despatch of the
Segestan envoys and the return visit of the Athenians in
416 B.C., and the final catastrophe of their Athenian allies
in 413.[16]

The Segestan piece that immediately concerns us is not
the earliest tetradrachm type of that city, but neither is it
the latest.   On the one hand we find the same reverse die
with which it is coupled also associated with a very different head of the Nymph, belonging properly to a didrachm
type and of rude transitional workmanship.[17]   On the
other hand there is extant a later version of the design of
the youthful River-God Krimisos, associated with a galloping quadriga, on a tetradrachm, which probably represents
the latest issue of the kind at Segesta.[18]   We shall not

---

[15] Thuc. *Hist.* vi., c. 46 ; and cf. Diodôros, lib. xii. c. 83.

[16] The sixty talents paid to the Athenians by the Segestans
before the expedition were, however, of uncoined silver (ἀσήμου
ἀργυρίου), Thuc. vi. 8.

[17] *B. M. Cat., Segesta,* No.30; Salinas, *Sul tipo de' tetradrammi
di Segesta,* Tav. 1. 3.   The highly interesting tetradrachm in the
De Luynes collection (Salinas, *op. cit.,* Tav. 1. 1, and p. 9, *seqq.*),
is also slightly earlier.   It shows the older epigraphic form
ΕΓΕＳΤΑΙΟΝ.

[18] *B. M. Cat., Segesta,* No. 31; Salinas, *op. cit.,* Tav. 1. 4—10.

therefore be far wrong in fixing the years 415 or 414 as
the approximate date of the piece under discussion; and
whether the obverse die of this coin was executed by
Evænetos himself or one of his pupils, this chronological
datum has, as already noticed,[19] an important retrospective
bearing on the date of the early Syracusan tetradrachm
of that artist. For it is certain that, whoever was the
actual engraver of the die, the design itself stands in a
filial relation to his Syracusan type. A certain advance
in style, the greater development of the hair, the new
form of earring, are so many indications that some
years at least had elapsed between the engraving of
Evænetos' early head of Arethusa and its Segestan copy.
In presence of this beautiful head of the Nymph Segesta,
we feel ourselves indeed much nearer the later version
of Arethusa, if Arethusa it be that occurs with Evænetos'
signature on the gold hundred-litra pieces of Syracuse,
executed, as we shall see, not long after the Athenian defeat.
This Segestan work, of which it may at least be said that
it belongs to the school of Evænetos, is indeed of extreme
utility in enabling us to bridge over his earlier and his
later "manner," and to supply a tolerably consecutive
art-history of this engraver. Of the importance of this
Segestan coin in its bearing on the earliest dekadrachm
type of Kimôn, with which it also presents so many
points in common, enough perhaps has been said in the
preceding section.[20]

Apart from the possibility of his having worked for
Segesta, the activity of Evænetos at Katanê during the
period which includes the Athenian siege sufficiently
accounts for the break in this engraver's connexion

---

[19] See p. 55.   [20] See p. 56.

with the Syracusan mint. If Segesta was the original ally and inviter of the Athenians, Katanê became throughout the period of hostilities an Athenian place of arms. There is quite enough therefore in the circumstances of the times to account for the detention of Evænetos, far longer than he himself may have desired, outside the walls of the great Sicilian city which had been the scene of his earliest as it was to be of his latest work.

In 409 B.C. peace was formally concluded between Syracuse and Katanê, and it is a significant fact that about this date Evænetos appears once more at Syracuse, as the engraver of the dies for the new gold coinage.

This new gold coinage consisted of pieces of two denominations; the larger, representing a silver value of a hundred litras, and the halves of the same of a gold value equivalent to the silver "medallions" or *pentēkonta-litra*.[21] The hundred-litra pieces (Pl. V. figs. 1—3)[22] present on their obverse a head of Arethusa in the star-spangled sphendonê, the earliest of which very closely approach the head of the same Nymph on Kimôn's earliest medallions of the higher relief (Type II.), struck, as we

---

[21] Head, *Coins of Syracuse*, p. 20.

[22] A hoard containing some fine specimens of these gold coins has recently been discovered at Avola, in Sicily, and published by Herr Arthur Löbbecke (*Münzfund von Avola in Zeitschr. f. Num.* 1890, p. 167 *seqq.*) Thanks to the kindness of Mr. H. Montagu, I am able to reproduce in Pl. V. figs. 1 and 2, two fine gold staters of Evænetos from this hoard, which are now in his Cabinet. Many have been acquired by the British Museum. According to my own information more than one find has been discovered in the same Sicilian district within the last few years, and I have myself seen specimens of two hoards of very different composition, one apparently dating from the early part of the Fourth Century and the other from the beginning of the Third. The coins described by Herr Löbbecke

have seen,[23] from about 410 B.C. onwards. From the signatures that accompany them it appears that both Kimôn
and Evænetos contributed towards producing these dies.
The signatures appear in the forms EYAI, EYAINE,[24]
K, and KI, and are always on the obverse side. The
civic name appears on one of the coins signed by Kimôn,[25]
in the earlier form ≤YPA KO≤ION, but otherwise the
Ω is always present. The form of the earring also varies.
On some pieces it is a single drop, as on Kimôn's later
"medallions." On the greater number of coins, however, the triple pendant is found. The pellets and star
which at times accompany the obverse head exhibit a
parallelism with some of the silver dekadrachm types of
Evænetos;[26] and this, as well as the development per-

---

seem to me to belong to two distinct hoards, one of early gold
coins including, besides the Syracusan, staters of Lampsakos and
Abydos and a Persian Daric: the other of late silver coins,
Pegasi, &c. Many gold coins of Agathoklês and Hiketas were
also found here about the same time as the early staters, but
these seem to have belonged to a third and still later hoard.

[23] See pp. 67 and 82.

[24] The legend EYAINE occurs on an example in the Cabinet
des Médailles, Paris, published by the Duc de Luynes, *Rev.
Num.* 1840, p. 21. Comparing this with another hundred-
litra piece in the same collection with the signature (KI) of
Kimôn, the Duc de Luynes observes: "Identiques pour le
type ces deux statères, gravés, sans doute, en concurrence par
les premiers artistes de Syracuse, offrent pourtant toute la
différence de relief, de pose, de tête, et de traits que l'on observe
entre les médaillons d'Evænète et ceux de Cimon."

[25] *B. M. Cat.*, Sicily, p. 170, No. 168.

[26] On one gold piece (*Annuaire de Numismatique*, 1868, Pl.
III.) two pellets are seen, which Head (*Coins of Syracuse*, p. 20)
with great probability takes to stand for two dekadrachms. On
some silver dekadrachms of Evænetos a single pellet is seen, as
if indicating the half of the gold coin. It is evident therefore
that the issue of these gold hundred-litra pieces overlapped that
of Evænetos' silver *pentékontalitra*.

ceptible in style, shows that these gold hundred-litra
pieces continued to be issued for a certain number of
years. Of the gold staters of Evœnetos those with the
star behind the head (Pl. V. fig. 1), which, although
unsigned, must in all probability be attributed to this
artist, are unquestionably the earliest. They present, as
will be shown, a remarkable parallelism in style with his
earliest "medallions." The latest type (Pl. V. fig. 3) is
executed in his most modern manner and displays his
signature.

The reverse of these gold staters represents a noble
design of Hêraklês strangling the Nemean lion, which
seems to betray the influence of a great work by Myrôn.
No signature is attached to this design, and we can only
infer that some dies are from the hand of Kimôn and
some from that of Evænetos.

The halves of the larger pieces, or gold *pentêkontalitra*,
show on one side a young male head, evidently of a River-
God—whether Anapos or Assinaros it might be hard to
determine—and on the other a free horse on a kind of
double base. From the **E** which occasionally appears
behind the head (cf. Pl. V. fig. 4), it is evident that
Evœnetos engraved some, at least, of the dies.

The appearance of the free horse upon these coins is
itself a most valuable indication as to date. By the
analogy of the later coins of Syracuse, in which the same
device is coupled with the head of Zeus Eleutherios, and
which belong to the days of the later Democracy,[27] we are

---

[27] I have elsewhere brought forward reasons for believing
that this type belongs to the time of Alexander the Molossian's
expedition (*Horsemen of Tarentum*, p. 83). The cult of Zeus
Eleutherios, however, had been introduced into Syracuse as
early as 466 B.C., on the exile of Thrasybulos and the estab-

naturally led to associate this type with the democratic
outburst that followed at Syracuse on the defeat of the
Athenians, and which took concrete shape in the banishment of Hermokratês and the aristocratic leaders, and the
revision of the constitution by Dioklês.[28]   The contemporary type of Hêraklês strangling the lion, also in all
probability, contains a speaking allusion to the liberation
from the great danger of foreign dominion that had
threatened Syracuse and Sicily.   At a little later date,
indeed, we find a similar design appearing on the federal
coins of the Italiote Greeks, with a direct reference to the
strife against their common enemies.   As a symbol of
alliance, moreover, the actual design as it occurs on the
Syracusan hundred-litra pieces was copied on a silver stater
of Tarsos (Pl. V. fig. 8), and another of Mallos, in Cilicia,
belonging to the period between the Persian dominion
and that of the Seleukids.[29]   The obverse of the coin of
Tarsos represents a female head of Hêra in a stephanos
adorned with an *anthêmion*—an offshoot of the Argive
type—accompanied by the legend **TEPΣIKON**.   That
of Mallos displays a head of Zeus, laurel-crowned, and,
according to the Duc de Luynes, the reverse of both
pieces, representing Hêraklês strangling the lion, is from

---

lishment at that time of a democratic government. (Diod.,
xi. 72.)

[28] I observe that Mr. Head (*Coins of Syracuse*, p. 20), though
he was inclined to place the issue of these gold pieces under
Dionysios, was so far impressed with the same argument that
he writes, " The type is more appropriate to the Democracy than
to the Tyranny of Dionysios ; possibly the dies were engraved
shortly before his accession, but as it has the Ω it is not likely
to be much earlier than 406."

[29] Duc de Luynes, *Essai sur la Numismatique des Satrapies et
de la Phénicie*, p. 62 ; Suppl. Pl. XI. (Wt. 10·50 grammes ;
Cabinet des Médailles.)

the same die, a remarkable evidence of a monetary conven-
tion between the two cities.[30]

That, as a matter of fact, the earliest of these gold pieces
date back to the Democratic period that succeeded the
Athenian siege is shown by a remarkable, though hitherto
neglected, piece of evidence. The free horse, namely,
on the gold fifty-litra pieces, above described, with the
curious double base below, supplied the design for some of
the earliest Carthaginian tetradrachms struck in Sicily,
which, as already stated, must be referred to the date of
Hannibal the son of Giskôn's expedition. It is highly
probable that this early Carthag'nian coinage for the use of
the mercenaries employed in Sicily was largely struck out
of the immense treasure acquired by the successive capture
of Selinûs and Himera, in 409 B.C., and shortly supplemented by that of Akragas and Gela. The immediate
occasion of it may well have been the equipment of the
second expedition under Hannibal and Himilkôn, just as
the preparation for the first Expedition seems to have
called forth the first "Carthaginian" issue of Motya and
Panormos. Up to this time Carthage had no coinage
of her own, and for a while her generals were content to
use the currency of her Phœnician dependents in the
Island. But the practice of her allies, the needs of her
Campanian mercenaries and the loot of the Greek cities
seem by the time of the Second Expedition to have suggested to her commanders the propriety of striking an
independent coinage with the name of Carthage. The
approximate date for the first coinage of these "Camp
Pieces" may be therefore set down as 406—5 B.C.[31]

---

[30] *Op. cit.* p. 62, "Même coin du revers que la médaille de
Tarse." (Wt. 10·27 grammes : De Luynes Coll.)

[31] See pp. 64, 67.

Of this early "Camp Coinage" there are two main types, both of which were well represented in the recent West-Sicilian find, described under Appendix A. These coins, which bear the legends *Machanat* (ﭏﻱﻩﻵ), or "the Camp," and *Kart-Chadasat* (ﭏﻱﭏﻩﻩﭏﻱﻩﭏ),[32] or "Carthage," show on their reverses the Phœnician palm-tree, but the obverse designs of both have a direct reference to the contemporary gold coinage of two Sicilian Greek cities, in the one case of Syracuse, in the other of Gela.

The obverse of one of these Carthaginian types represents a free horse galloping to the left and crowned by a flying Victory (Pl. V. fig. 10), and, though the Victory is absent on the Syracusan piece, the horse itself is a very exact reproduction of that which appears on the gold dekadrachms of Syracuse already referred to. That it is, in fact, taken from the Syracusan coin appears from the further reproduction of the double-lined base, or two-fold exergual line which is seen beneath the horse on the Syracusan original, and which on the Punic copy serves at times to contain the inscription *Kart-Chadasat*, in the same position as the ϹYPAKOϹIΩN on some of the Syracusan originals. A double exergual line is itself so exceptional a phenomenon that its appearance beneath the horse in both designs, as well as its connexion with the legend, affords a clear indication that one is taken from the other. A similar indebtedness is also shown by a Siculo-Punic didrachm[33] with the inscription "Ziz," and in this case, moreover, the youthful male head on the obverse was evidently suggested by that of the River-God on the Syracusan *pentēkontalitron*.

---

[32] L. Müller, *Numismatique de l'ancienne Afrique*, vol. ii., p. 74, 75.

[33] *B. M. Cat.*, *Sicily*, p. 248, No. 20.

On the other main type of these early Carthaginian tetra-drachms the free horse is replaced by the forepart of a horse, usually equipped with a bridle, the loop of which curves up in a curious way behind his head (Fig. 8). This type, in its turn, recalls the half horse with a looped bridle on a gold litra of Gela, the obverse side of which displays a head of Persephonê and the inscription ƧΩƧI-ΓΟΛΙƧ (Fig 7).[34] This small Gelan coin is the half of a better-known gold *dilitron* having a whole horse on its reverse, and, taking the proportion of gold to silver as 15 to 1, the two coins respectively represent silver values of six and three drachmæ.

It will be seen that the half horse on this Gelan coin has a real significance, indicating, according to a well-

Fig. 7.—Gold Litra of Gela.   (2 diams.)

established rule of the Greek monetary system, that it is the half of the larger piece representing the complete animal. On the Gelan piece, again, in conformity with the half bull which is the usual type of the city and stands for the river-god Gelas, the half horse is repre-sented as swimming rather than galloping, and this peculi-arity of the motive seems slightly to have affected the

---

[34] This coin, of which I obtained a specimen from the site of the Greek cemetery at Gela (Terranova), a vineyard of Sig. E. Lauricella, in 1888, is of the greatest rarity, and has not been described by any author since an indifferent engraving of it appeared in Castelli's work (Auct. II. *Gelensium*). It weighs 13½ grains (cf. p. 63). A forgery of this type is known, with a much coarser head and in higher relief, a specimen of which was sold in the York Moore' sale.

forelegs of the horse on some of the Carthaginian coins. The grain of barley here seen either before or above the horse is evidently taken from the contemporary tetra-drachms of Gela, where it appears above the bull. It is highly probable that this issue was struck out of bullion acquired by the capture of Gela in 405 B.C.

It is evident that the Carthaginian moneyers, in attaching this half horse with the looped bridle to their new dies, were simply transferring a design from a place where it had an obvious meaning to a place where it has no special appropriateness. The Gelan gold litra is the original, and the Siculo-Punic tetradrachm is the copy, finely executed, indeed, and by a skilled Greek hand.

Fig. 8.—Carthaginian "Camp-Piece" (Tetradrachm).

We thus acquire a useful analogy for the contemporary imitation of the small Syracusan gold piece. From this Gelan parallel, as well as on the ground of general proba-bility, we are entitled to infer that in this case, too, the design on the Greek coins is the original, and the Punic a copy.[35]

---

[35] That the Carthaginian moneyers should have thus selected the horse and half horse for imitation on their coinage was probably not due to arbitrary causes. The horse seems to have had a special significance in their eyes as a Libyan emblem (cf. *Movers, Phönizier*, ii. 1, p. 4; Müller, *Num. de l'ancienne Afrique*, ii. 115); and perhaps as consecrated to the God of the Sea. On many Siculo-Punic and Carthaginian coins, however, it is undoubtedly associated with symbols of Baal and Ashtoreth.

It thus appears that some at least of the gold fifty and hundred-litra pieces of Syracuse were already in circulation before the date of the first issue of these Carthaginian "Camp Coins," which, as has been shown, may be approximately set down as 406—5 B.C. On the other hand, from the fact that upon these coins, with very few exceptions, the earring with its triple pendant already occurs, it is probable that they were not issued much earlier than this date.

In close connection with these Punic tetradrachms, and attesting the same Syracusan influences, must also be mentioned two extremely rare Punic gold pieces (Pl. V., fig. 12), weighing respectively 117·9 [36] and 23 grs. [37] Both these coins exhibit an obverse head of Dêmêtêr, with a single-drop earring wreathed with ears of barley, which seems to show the influence both of the gold hundred-litra pieces of Evænetos and of his silver "medallions," with the head of Korê. [38] They bear at the same time on their reverse a free horse on a double-lined base, evidently derived from the reverse design on the fifty-litra gold piece by the same artist, though here consecrated, as it would seem, to the Phœnician divinity by the symbol 🜨, placed in the field above it. From the superior style of

---

[36] Müller (Num. de l'anc. Afrique, ii. p. 86, No. 74). The single example cited is in the B. M. Another variety exists without the symbol. Both are Phœnician staters (Müller, No. 75).

[37] In the B. M. a smaller gold coin also exists, with a similar head and a horse's head on the rev. Müller, op. cit. ii. p. 87, No. 77 (Weight, 1·57 — 1·52 grammes).

[38] A Siculo-Punic tetradrachm, with the inscription, Kart-Chadasat (Müller, op. cit. p. 74, 1; Head, Coins of the Ancients, Pl. XXVI. 39) shows an obverse head of the same type, but with an earring of three pendants in place of a single drop, which betrays the later fashion. The reverse, a horse standing in front of a palm-tree, fits on to a somewhat later series of Siculo-Punic coins.

these coins, which separate them *longo intervallo* from the later gold and electrum series of Carthage, it is evident that, like the tetradrachms with the similar reverse type, they must be referred to the earliest period of Carthaginian coinage in Sicily. In this case, the first appearance of the head of Dêmêtêr on a coin struck by Carthaginian authority was, in all probability, anterior by a few years at least to the outrage on her Syracusan sanctuary that evoked the special expiatory cult of the Goddess at Carthage itself.

There is nothing, at least, in such a supposition that need surprise us. The Hellenization both of Carthage itself and its dependencies in the Island had by this date reached such a pitch that the acceptance by them of the cult of the presiding divinities of Sicily was only to be expected. The head of Arethusa, on one side of her mythical being more of a Goddess than a Nymph, had already been copied at Motya and Panormos. Nay, more, we know that as early as 480 B.C. Gelôn had required the Carthaginians to build two temples, which could not well be other than those of " the Goddesses," in which the stones were to be preserved whereon the treaty was graven.[39]

Both the fact that the cult of Dêmêtêr and her Daughter was probably of old standing at Carthage at this date, and the actual appearance of the head of the Mother Goddess on Carthaginian gold types presumably anterior to 396 B.C., bring into relief a negative phenomenon which the recently discovered West Sicilian hoard [40]

---

[39] Diod. xi. 26. Freeman, *Sicily*, ii. 210, remarks: " These could not fail to be temples to Greek deities ; we may say almost with certainty that they were temples to the goddesses of Sicily, the special patronesses of Gelôn and his house, Dêmêtêr and the Korê."

[40] See Appendix A.

establishes with great precision. In that hoard, withdrawn from circulation about 400 B.C., the early "Camp coinage" of Carthage in the Island, presenting the horse and half horse, together with the contemporary or slightly earlier issues of the old Phœnician settlements Motya and Panormos, was brilliantly represented.[41] There occurred a "medallion" in Kimôn's later style (Type II.), slightly used, and three early "medallions" of Evænetos in brilliant condition; but whereas among the Phœnician coins of Motya and those inscribed *Ziz*, which must probably be referred to the Panormitis, there were, as already mentioned in the section on Kimôn, a series of imitations of the earlier "medallion" types of that artist,[42] not a single example occurred of a Siculo-Punic coin-type imitated from the Korê head of Evænetos, though we know that at a slightly later date this magnificent design took, as it were, the Punic world by storm. In the absence of any religious reason for not copying this type, which, as we have seen, there is no warrant for supposing, the inevitable conclusion to which we are led is, that at the time when, in 410—8 B.C., this class of Motyan and Panormitic coins first issued from the mint, the silver dekadrachms of Evænetos had not yet made their appearance. In this department Kimôn still held the field.

On the other hand, it does not seem safe to bring down the first issue of Evænetos' "medallions" many years below this date. From the fact that two fine specimens of Evænetos' dekadrachms were contained in the "West Sicilian" hoard, there is good reason for believing that their issue had begun some few years at least before 400 B.C. The gold hundred-litra pieces of Evænetos

---

supply a still more definite chronological indication. Just as the earliest of the gold staters presenting Kimôn's signature show an obvious analogy in style to his second type of silver dekadrachms,[43] so the earliest of those attributable to Evænetos connect themselves in the most evident manner with his early silver " medallions," exhibiting a cockle-shell behind the head of Korê (Pl. V., fig. 10). This is the "medallion" type the reverse of which, as already pointed out,[44] shows the nearest approach to that of the New Engraver, and which closest follows his work in date. If, then, as shown by their Carthaginian imitations dating from 406—5 B.C., the gold staters of Evænetos were struck by about 408 B.C., it becomes highly probable, on every ground, that the earliest "medallion" dies were engraved shortly after that date, say, by 406 B.C.

The date thus acquired for the first issue of the silver " medallions " of Evænetos agrees very well with the fact, deducible from the marks of value that occur on some of them,[45] that the coinage of the gold hundred-litra pieces seems to have to a certain extent overlapped that of these silver *pentékontalitra*. In the case of the gold coins two dots occasionally occur beside the head ; in the case of their silver halves a single dot.

The first appearance of Evænetos' splendid design of the head of Korê at the very beginning of the Dionysian Era fully agrees with the intimate relation in which it stands to the head of the same Goddess on the newly discovered "medallion," the issue of which has been referred to the same date as Kimôn's third "medallion" type, or approximately to the same year, 406 B.C.

Of the relation in which Evænetos' "medallion" type

---

stands to the work of the New Artist enough will have been said in the section devoted to that subject. As supplying a new standpoint for critically surveying the masterpiece of Evænetos, the new coin has an unique value. Especially does it bring into clear relief that artistic quality of Evænetos which led him, in his more modern presentation of the Korê, to subordinate details to the general effect, while the reverse type illustrates his singular ingenuity in bringing out by characteristic touches the most thrilling incidents in the chariot race.

In the " medallion " series of Evænetos himself there is distinct evidence of a progressive advance in style which is most palpably perceptible in the treatment of his chariot groups. The action of the horses on his earlier dies is much more even and level—far less sensational, indeed, than on the tetradrachms executed by him at a considerably earlier date. In this again, as suggested above, we may detect the sobering influence of the very regular and harmonious design in the "medallion" by the New Engraver. Upon the dekadrachms of Evænetos, however, the action of the horses becomes rapidly higher, till the foremost horses seem to break away from their fellows.

To attempt any exact chronology of these successive issues would be impossible with the data at our disposal. The variety of dies and the different symbols introduced, as well as the evidences of development in style, show that the coinage of the silver dekadrachms of Evænetos must have continued for a considerable number of years. Among the earliest types, after those with a cockle-shell behind the head of Korê (Pl. V. fig. 10), which must certainly claim precedence, are those which present a Δ (probably $= \Delta\epsilon\kappa\acute{a}\delta\rho\alpha\chi\mu o\nu$) in the field, and the signature

P

EYAINE beneath the neck (Pl. V. fig. 11). The latest is unquestionably the new type afforded by the Santa Maria di Licodia hoard, exhibiting the full signature in the later orthography **EYAINETOY**, beneath a head of abnormally small proportions[46] (Pl. V. fig. 13). From the evidence supplied by this find it appears that this latter coin must have been struck before the approximate date 380 B.C. If we allow a period of about twenty years for the engraving of Evænetos' "medallion" dies, it may have been struck as late as 385 B.C. From the oxidized or fractured state to which some of the dies had been reduced when many of the coins bearing his designs were struck, it appears, however, probable that they still continued in use at a time when, whether from death or old age or some other cause, the activity of Evænetos himself had ceased.[47] The fact, to which attention will be shortly called, that these fine coins continued to be imitated, both by Greeks and Carthaginians, down to the Third Century B.C., also tends to show that their circulation, if not their issue, continued to be fairly abundant for some time after the latest possible date at which their dies can have been engraved. This conclusion, as I hope to show, is of considerable importance in helping us to bridge over an extensive gap in the Syracusan coinage.

The appearance of the head of Dêmêtêr on the early Siculo-Punic gold pieces above referred to, is at most an isolated phenomenon. It does not exclude the main fact with which we have to deal,[48] namely, that the attempts made by Carthage to reconcile the offended Goddesses for

---

[46] See p. 22.   [47] See p. 20, 25.
[48] Diodôros xiv. 63 and 77. Cf. Müller, *op. cit.* ii. pp. 110, 111. Münter, *Religion des Carth.* p. 108; De Saulcy, *Acad. des Inscriptions*, T. XV. Pl. II. p. 53, 54.

the **profanation of their shrines** during the campaign **of** 396—4, **in** all probability explained the prominent place assumed by Dêmêtêr and her daughter on the later **Punic** coinages, both in Sicily and Africa.

The date of this solemn propitiation may, perhaps, be approximately set down as 393 B.C., and it is some time after this that the brilliant series of tetradrachms presenting obverse **heads copied** from the Korê of Evænetos' medallions **makes** its first appearance from the Siculo-Punic dies. **The** bulk of these coins belongs, indeed, to a considerably later date, and they are **of** decidedly later style than the **coins** presenting the free or **half horse.** The **earliest are** accompanied on the reverse sides with a **quadriga and** the inscription *Ziz* (Pl. VII. fig. 2), **or by a horse in front of** a palm-tree without any **legend (Pl. VI. fig. 11).**

.**The** quadriga types **with which Evænetos' Korê is** coupled on the Carthaginian coins **of Sicily are generally** borrowed from those **of** Evænetos, and a good example **of** an imitation of the most sensational chariot group of that artist on a coin of Hêrakleia Minoa (*Rash Melkart*) will be seen on Pl. VII., fig. 13.   At times the head of the young **Goddess** on those Punic pieces is accompanied by symbols, such as the cockle-shell and the griffin's head, that are associated **with it on the** Syracusan medallions ; at times it is coupled with a *caduceus*,[49] a *thymiatèrion*, or a poppy-head, **and on one very beautiful type**[50] (Pl. VII.

---

[49] The symbol of *Taut-Cadmus*, the Egyptian *Thoth*, assimilated to Hermês.   Cf. Müller, *Num. de l'anc. Afr.* ii. p. 34.

[50] This coin, which appears to be unique, was recently obtained by me in Eastern Sicily. The same symbol, however, is also found on another variety (*B. M. Cat.*, *Sicily*, p. 248, No. 12) behind the head of Persephonê. This, like the other piece, is inscribed *Ziz*, and **must probably be assigned to** Panormos.

fig. 4) a *swastika* is placed in front of her lips.[51] This coin, which bears the inscription *Ziz* beneath the quadriga on the reverse, must probably be ascribed to Panormos, and the introduction of the *swastika* links it on to earlier coins of that city, in which the same symbol is placed beside an earlier female head, whether of **Nymph** or Goddess. At Eryx this *crux gammata* seems to be associated with the cult of her Aphroditê. The ⛨, which seems to be the special symbol of Baal-Chamman, also occurs, but it is **only found** coupled **with** the head which is crowned with ears of barley[52] in place of the green spray, and which, perhaps, therefore represents Dêmêtêr.

Of the Carthaginian "Camp coins" with **the** head of Evænetos' Korê, some **of** those presenting a horse's head **on the reverse are** unquestionably the latest, **for** they fit on to the tetradrachms bearing the Alexandrine type of the head of Hêraklês or Melkart. It thus appears that the imitation of Evænetos' type by the Punic moneyers of Sicily continued till at least as late as 330 B.C.

From the Camp pieces struck by the Carthaginians in Sicily for their mercenaries and dependents in the island, Evænetos' famous type spread in a modified form to Carthage herself. **In this case, on** some of the Siculo-Punic coins already referred to, and notably the early gold staters with the free horse, the Goddess is represented rather under the aspect of **the** Mother than of the Daughter, with the ears of ripened corn in place of the green barley spray of spring. (Pl. VII., fig. 5.)

The type, thus derived, becomes, from the middle of the **Fourth Century onwards, the** unvarying badge of the

---

[51] It is seen above **the hound on the reverse** of some small silver coins of Eryx (*B. M. Cat. Eryx*, Nos. 10-12).

[52] *E.g.* Müller, *op. cit.* ii. p. 77, No. 32.

Carthaginian coinage in all metals.[53]   As compared with
the earlier Siculo-Punic copies of Evænetos' Korê, the
style of these coins is hard and mechanical, but some
elements in the original design, such as the curving
barley-leaf that shoots across the hair, are curiously per-
sistent, and the Gaulish tribes, with whom the gold and
electrum staters of Carthage must have gained a considerable currency, seem to have incorporated this horn-
like appendage as a decorative adjunct to more than one
of their hybrid coin-types.   It is to this source that we
may venture to trace the curious ornament that crosses
the locks of the composite head on the gold and electrum
pieces of Belgic Gaul, and the final degeneration of which
may be surveyed on the Ancient British coin-types.[54]

The long supremacy of Evænetos' design at Syracuse
itself is shown by its imitation on a whole series of later
issues.   Not to speak of its appearance on some small
copper coins,[55] with Pegasos on the reverse, struck about
Timoleôn's time, it was revived, in a fine style for
the period, on the tetradrachms struck in the earlier

---

[53] See Ludwig Müller, *Num. de l'Afrique Ancienne*, vol. ii. p.
84—115.

[54] The source of this is most clearly seen in some hybrid
gold coins found in Picardy (*Rev. Num.* 1883, Pl. I. figs. 1, 2),
the reverse types of which, as has been recognized by M.
Anatole de Barthélemy (*op. cit.* p. 8) are imitated from gold
staters of Tarentum.   The head is in this case combined in a
remarkable way with a prancing horse, more suggestive of the
silver types of Carthage.   These coins seem to me to supply
the missing link between the curious hair ornament of the
characteristic Belgic types and the curling barley-leaf of the
Carthaginian staters.   My Father (*Coins of the Ancient Britons*,
Supplement, p. 424) has not seen his way to adopt this suggestion; it has, however, been approved by Mr. Head (*Num. Chron.*,
1890, p. 331).

[55] Head, *Coins of Syracuse*, p. 31, Pl. VI.

years of Agathoklês' reign (Pl. VI. fig. 2), in this instance coupled with a reverse type borrowed from Kimón's "medallions."[56] On the later coins of Agathoklês it is succeeded by the new and more youthful presentment of the Maiden Goddess, bearing the inscription **KOPA** behind her head,[57] but, in spite of her flowing tresses, the influence of the older design is still perceptible. Once more, upon the gold staters of Hiketas (287—278 B.C.) Evænetos' type was again elaborately copied (Pl. VI. fig. 3),[58] though the ear of barley that here shoots forth from the wreath seems more appropriate to Dêmêtêr than to her daughter; and it appears at Syracuse for the last time on some bronze pieces of Hierón II. (B.C. 275—216).[59]

The appearance of a head of Korê, in its essential lines identical with Evænetos' design, but in a bolder style in harmony with the art traditions of Greece proper, on didrachms of the Opuntian Locrians [60] (Pl. VI. figs. 1, 2),

---

[56] Head, *Coins of Syracuse*, p. 43, Pl. VIII. 4.
[57] *Op. cit.*, Pl. IX. 1, 2.
[58] *Op. cit.*, Pl. X. 1, 2.
[59] *Op. cit.*, Pl. XII. 6.
[60] Mr. Head (*B. M. Cat.*, *Central Greece*, p. xv.) says of the coinage of Opus, that "we may rest assured that it is all subsequent to the Peace of Antalkidas (B.C. 387)," and he refers the introduction of the types with the head of Persephonê to the year 369, in which year Dionysios took part in the Peace Congress that met at Delphi. It is to the same, or the succeeding year, which marks the restoration of the Messenians, that the issue of the Messenian didrachm with a similar head of Korê must unquestionably be referred (cf. Gardner, *B. M. Cat.*, *Peloponnese*, p. xliii.). That these pieces mark the date of the restoration of the Messenians and the foundation of Messene by Epaminondas may be admitted. On the other hand, the intervention of Dionysios in the affairs of the mother-country had been consistently pro-Spartan. It is possible, therefore, that the adoption of Evænetos' type, to illustrate the old Messenian cult of Persephonê on the coins of the newly founded city, may, after all, be a purely artistic tribute.

Pheneates[61] (Pl. VI. fig. 4), and Messenians[62] (Pl. VI. fig. 3), is a striking witness to its early popularity. It is to be observed in this connexion that a further numismatic link between these Opuntian dies and those of the Syracusan engravers is to be found in the figure of Ajax, which accompanies the reverse of the type in question, and which unmistakeably corresponds with the Leukaspis as he appears on some Syracusan drachmæ executed by the earlier master Eumenês[63] and, with some variations, by his pupil, Eukleidas.[64]

Evænetos' head of Persephonê is found about the same date on coins of Pheræ in Thessaly and Knôssos in Crete. In Sicily itself a fine reproduction of it occurs on the large bronze pieces of Kentoripa (Pl. VI. fig. 4), where the types are overstruck on Syracusan coins representing a head of Pallas.[65] The pard on the reverse of this Kentoripan coin is also a very beautiful work.

On the mainland of Italy the Korê of the Syracusan master seems to have affected more than one of the beautiful didrachm types of Metapontion; sometimes with the addition of the ear of corn and the diaphanous Tarentine veil, taking the form of Dêmêtêr;[66] sometimes in her own person as the Daughter, though here with more flowing hair, as

---

[61] *B. M. Cat.*, *Peloponnese*, Pl. XXXV. 7; Gardner, *Types of Greek Coins*, Pl. VIII. 41, and p. 155.

[62] *B. M. Cat.*, *Peloponnese*, Pl. XXI. 1.

[63] *B. M. Cat.*, No. 162; Head, *Coins of Syracuse*, Pl. III. 15; Weil, *Künstlerinschriften*, &c., Taf. i. 3.

[64] *B. M. Cat.*, Nos. 226—230; Head, *op. cit.*, Pl. V. 6.

[65] Head, *Coins of Syracuse*, Pl. VIII. 1. I have elsewhere (p. 159) pointed out that this type is considerably earlier than Timoleôn's time.

[66] Carelli, *Num. Ital. Vet.*, T. clii. 69, 70, 73, &c. Cf. Garrucci, *Le Monete d'Italia Antica*, T. ciii. 5.

on the later Syracusan version **cited above.**[67] On the Third **Century** didrachms of Arpi, **in Apulia, it is more** literally reproduced,[68] though probably from an Agathokleian copy.

At Massalia Evœnetos' masterpiece stood as the model for the **fine** head of Artemis upon its drachms (Pl. VI. fig. 8)[69] struck about the middle of the Fourth Century B.C., though here an olive-wreath takes the place of the barley. In a more literal guise it passed to the coin-types of the **daughter** colony, Rhoda, on the Pyrenœan coast of **Spain (Pl. VI. fig. 9),**[70] and, **perhaps** through a Siculo-Punic intermediary, to those of the sister colony of Emporiœ (Pl. VI. fig. 10).[71] From these Greek plantations of the "Spanish March" the type **was received** and reproduced **by** the neighbouring Iberic **and** Gaulish tribes of **Aqui-**tania[72] in a series of imitations, each more barbarous than **the last, and, passing thence in a** half-dissected form

---

[67] Carelli, *Num. Ital. Vet.*, clii. 74, 81, **&c.** Cf. Garrucci, *Le Monete d'Italia Antica*, T. ciii. 21, &c.

[68] Carelli, *op. cit.*, xc. 1—3; Garrucci, *op. cit.*, xciii. 1.

[69] Cf. De la Saussaye, *Numismatique de la Gaule Narbonnaise*, Pl. II. 54—57, &c.

[70] Heiss, *Monnaies Antiques de l'Espagne*, Pl. I., *Rhoda*, 1—8.

[71] Duc de Luynes, *Rev. Num.* 1840, 5 *seqq.*; Heiss, *Monnaies Antiques de l'Espagne*, Pl. I., *Emporiœ*, 1—10.

[72] Cf. De Saulcy, *Rev. Num.* iv. 1867, p. 1 *seqq.*; De la Saussaye :—*Monnaies épigraphiques des Volces Tectosages* (*Rev. Num.* 1866, p. 389—401); Maxe-Werly, *Rev. Num.* 1886, p. 1 *seqq.* ("Petrocorii," &c.), and *Rev. Belge de Num.* 1879, p. 248 *seqq.* ("Trouvaille de Cuzance," &c., "Cadurci"); E. Hucher, *L'Art Gaulois*, Pt. II. p. 31, &c. **The** evolution of these types in their Northern and Western progress is a curious study, but it cannot here **be followed out in** detail. I regard the triple crest **above the head** on so many Armorican coins (by Hucher fantasti-**cally** connected with Ogmios) as ultimately due to the locks and sprays of the Syracusan Korê, introduced North of the Pyrenees principally by **the Rhodan** currency. For good intermediate examples compare the **coins of the** Petrocorii and Volcœ Tectosages.

through Quercy and Perigord to the Limousin, supplied some characteristic elements to the coin-types of the North and West. The curving barley-sprays above the forehead and twined amidst the tresses of our Persephonê, the twin fishes in front of her lips, were drawn out into fantastic crests and scrolls upon the coin-types of Armorica, and the remote descendants of the dolphins that once sported in the Great Harbour of Syracuse were finally stranded upon the Western shores of our own Island. Upon some late British silver-types [73] of the First Century of our era, the range of which extends from Plymouth to Tewkesbury and Oxford, they may still be traced before a grotesque profile which may well be taken to represent the extreme link of the chain that leads back to the masterpiece of Evænetos, and through him to the beautiful creation of the New Engraver.

A more purely artistic tribute to the abiding popularity of Evænetos' head of Persephonê, as she appears on his "medallions," is supplied from a source to which we should otherwise hardly look for numismatic illustration. A reduced copy, namely, of this head of Korê, appears on a series of *kylikes*, of a thin black-coloured pottery, with a lustrous metallic glaze, belonging to a well-marked class of ceramic ware intended to imitate silver vessels. The fabric of this class of pottery seems to have attained considerable dimensions in Sicily and Great Greece in the Third Century B.C.; [74] the shallow two-handled bowls in

---

[73] J. Evans, *Coins of the Ancient Britons*, Pl. F. 4—8; and cf. p. 106.

[74] Some are probably earlier. I recently obtained at Catania, for the Ashmolean Museum, an *askos* or *guttus* of this ware, with a head, perhaps of Apollo, in a Late Transitional style of art. Even supposing the stamp to have been taken from earlier work, such a Transitional model would hardly have been

which the head of Evænetos' Persephonê forms the central relief, was, however, a specially Campanian fabric, and all the examples known to me, of which the exact find-spot was recorded, were found in the neighbourhood of Capua. The central relief of these *kylikes* has a distinct margin, and bears evidence of having been inserted after the cup itself was turned. The impression had therefore been first produced on a separate clay disk. And as no doubt a clay stamp was used like that from the Castellani Collection in the British Museum for a similar purpose, a double shrinkage in the design was the result, produced, first, by the drying of the original stamp, and secondly, by the drying of its impression on the clay disk. In this way the "medallion" reliefs, as seen upon the cups, have lost about a third of their diameter, and give the idea of tetra-drachms, of which no examples with Evænetos' Korê head are known, rather than of dekadrachms.

That the original stamp was actually moulded on Evænetos' "medallions" there can, however, in spite of this apparent discrepancy in module, be no doubt. Although from the imperfect character of the clay impressions much of the delicate engraving is lost, enough remains to show

---

selected in the Third Century. The prototype of this looks as if it had been a Leontine coin of abnormal module. Unfortunately, however, no Sicilian coins of such calibre are known to us. Silver *kylikes*, analogous to those imitated, but without the central medallion, have been found in Pantikapæan tombs of the Fourth Century B.C. A silver bowl, with a beautiful medallion relief of a Mænad in the centre, of Hellenistic work, was recently found at Taranto, though, with the exception of the central relief (now in Dr. J. Evans's collection), it crumbled to dust, owing to the thinness of the plate. A silver prototype of the well-known Cales-ware bowls, with chariot-racing scenes, is in the British Museum. Mr. C. Smith regards it as of Campanian fabric of the Third Century B.C.

that the stamp was taken from the coins themselves, and not from any Third Century copies or reductions. The whole expression of the face, as much as the arrangement of the hair, shows that we have to do, in a doubly reflected form, it is true, with the actual handiwork of Evænetos. As a matter of fact an examination of these *kylikes* has enabled me to detect three variations of the dekadrachm designs of this artist, in some cases, moreover, authenticated by traces of his signature.[75]

The varieties used are :—

1. The dekadrachm represented on Pl. V. fig. 11, with the Δ in the field beneath the chin of Persephonê, the dekadrachm mark being well preserved. On one of these impressions the signature [E]YAINE is clearly visible.[76]

2. The dekadrachm, Pl. V. fig. 10, without the Δ but with a cockle-shell behind the head.[77]

3. Without symbol or letter (cf., Pl. V. fig. 12). On an impression of this type traces of the letters EYAI .. are visible.[78]

---

[75] In the same way the signature of Eukleidas may be traced on the helmet of a three-quarter facing head of Pallas on a paste disk, in the British Museum taken from a mould of his celebrated tetradrachm. This disk was no doubt intended to be attached to the centre of a glass vessel in the same manner as the clay disks with Evænetos' design. It may be observed in this connexion that glass imitations of metallic forms are not infrequent.

[76] Two examples of *kylikes* with this "medallion" type are in the Ashmolean Museum, both found at or near Capua. That with the signature was presented by the Rev. G. J. Chester, the other is from the Fortnum Collection.

[77] One example from Capua is in the Ashm. Mus.; another, the source of which is not indicated, in the Brit. Mus.; a third (Campana Collection " S. Italy ") in the Louvre; a fourth is in the possession of Messrs. Rollin and Feuardent at Paris.

[78] In the British Museum.

There is besides a class of *kylikes* with very barbarous imitations of the central medallion.[79]

This interesting ceramic class, in which both the form, the central design, and the metallic lustre are imitated from silver work, presupposes the existence of a special class of ancient silver vessels of the kind, with actual medallions of Evænetos inserted in their central ornament; just as Imperial *aurei* are seen set round the famous *patera* of Rennes, or, to take a more modern example, we may see a crown-piece of Charles II. inserted in the middle of a punch-bowl. These Capuan *kylikes*, in short, represented a cheap popular substitute for what was evidently a famous and highly-prized form of Syracusan plate.

And in view of this special association of Evænetos "medallions" with silversmith's work, we are tempted to make the further suggestion that Evænetos himself also practised the toreutic art. Considering, indeed, the natural combination of the two crafts in ancient and mediæval times, nothing can be more reasonable than to suppose that his ἀργυροκοπεῖον, like those of Antioch, frequented by Antiochos Epiphanês,[80] was in close connexion with a gold or silversmith's shop, and gave employment to *toreutæ* as well as die-sinkers. The gaps in the numismatic records of Evænetos' career clearly show that his activity was also occupied in other artistic directions.

---

[79] Two examples, both from Capua, are in the Ashm. Mus., another from a different stamp in the Louvre.

[80] *Athenæos*, lib. x. (on the authority of Polybios, *Hist. Reliq.* lib. xxvi. c. 7, 3). Cf. my *Horsemen of Tarentum* (London, Quaritch, 1889, p. 120 *seqq.*), where I have endeavoured to show that the ancient die-sinkers signed not only as artists, but in their quality of moneyers, and combined besides the kindred crafts of τορευτής and χρυσοχόος. The term ἀργυροκόπος seems to mean "silversmith" in general as well as "moneyer."

That Evænetos, as seems fairly ascertained in the case of his fellow die-sinker Phrygillos, also exercised the profession of a gem-engraver is made highly probable from the microscopic fineness that characterizes some of his earlier dies. Mr. Head,[81] indeed, remarks of Evænetos that "his work is characterized by an almost gem-like minuteness, which approaches to hardness." In surveying his designs we are often conscious of a hand somewhat over-familiar with the use of the diamond point. It seems possible, indeed, that an actual example of a gem engraved by this artist has survived to our day. A gold ring containing an exquisitely-engraved sard was recently discovered in the neighbourhood of Catania, and though the ignorant peasant who wished to realise the gold-value of the ring, and thought the stone of little value, broke it in two in tearing it from its socket, the intaglio, which has been preserved by a happy accident, has not suffered in any essential particular. The design, of which a phototype is given on Pl. V. fig. 5, represents Heraklês strangling the Nemean lion, and it will be seen to be almost identical in the minutest details with the reverse of Evænetos' gold hundred-litra piece placed next it on the plate. It is true that the same design, executed in an almost identical manner, occurs on the parallel gold staters from the hand of Kimôn, but a comparison between the impression of the gem on Pl. V., fig. 5, with the reverse of fig. 1, seems to show that the nearest correspondence in style is found with the work of Evænetos.

The only important point in which the design on the gem differs from the coins is, that here the struggling figures rest on a simple line, whereas on the coin-dies

---

[81] *Coins of Syracuse*, p. 22.

some indication of rocks, and, in one instance, of an ear of corn, is given below.

The style of workmanship on the **gem** is such as enables us to refer it to the close of the Fifth or the beginning of the Fourth Century B.C. The material, a brilliant sard, is worthy of the best days of Greek gem **engraving**; and the bold, though somewhat shallow, intaglio quite agrees with this conclusion. **The relief** on the coin is proportionally somewhat higher than that on the impression from the gem, a relative proportion generally maintained in contemporary **works** in the two materials belonging to this age. **The softer material** of the **die as** compared with the stone **seems** to have tempted deeper incision; but in other respects the technique **is** strikingly similar. **We see** in the gem, as in the die, the same firm, sure incision of a master of the glyptic art ; and in the design itself, the same unique combination **of the** utmost delicacy **of detail with** the full expression of the mighty forces pitted against each other in the struggling group **of hero and lion.**

The correspondence between the design on **the signet and** that on the coins places this intaglio **in a** rare, but **well-marked class of** ancient gems which reproduce civic **badges, and which** undoubtedly were used by officers of **the State to seal** public Acts. **On** the present occasion it is impossible to do more than to call attention to the existence of this special class of gems, which **well** deserve a separate treatise.

It may be sufficient here to notice that several examples of these **civic** signets are forthcoming engraved with the same official types that reappear **on** the coinage of Greek cities of Sicily, **and of Great Greece. One** of the most important of these, recently obtained by me from Sicily, represents the *protomé* of the man-faced bull of Gela, its body countermarked by a Corinthian helmet which was evidently a magistrate's symbol ;[82] and a cut scarab in the British Museum displays the legend ΓΕΛΑΣ above a man-headed bull between a flower and star, with a snake below.[83] Another gem in the British Museum recalls the Nymph and swan of the early coins of Kamarina. At Selinûs we have the evidence of the existence of similar signets in some remarkable clay impressions found in Temple C. of the Acropolis.[84] One of the two most numerously reproduced of the seals represented in this deposit exhibits the type of Hêraklês struggling with the tauriform River-God, which, in an earlier guise, is found upon the didrachms of Selinûs, and the civic and official character of the signet gem—δημοσία σφραγίς— was in this case further authenticated by a large Σ in

[82] A phototype of this gem is published in Imhoof-Blumer und Otto Keller, *Tier- und Pflanzenbilder auf Münzen und Gemmen* (Taf. xxvi. 45), with the remark : "Schöner Stil. Wahrscheinlich das Siegel eines griechischen Ritters der besten Zeit." Owing to some misunderstanding of the account supplied by me it is here described as from "Tarentum." I obtained it, however, from Sicily, which makes it the more improbable that it was a private seal. From Salona, in Dalmatia, I have a cornelian gem with the Knidian Aphroditê and the legend KOPINΘOY, evidently a Corinthian official seal.

[83] *B. M. Cat. of Gems*, 444 ; and cf. Imhoof-Blumer und Keller, *op. cit.*, Taf. xxvi. 47.

[84] They have been published by Prof. Salinas in the *Notizie degli Scavi* (1883, p. 281 *seqq.*, and Tav. vii., xv.), and are preserved in the Museum of Palermo. Six hundred and forty-three were found in all. The type of Hêraklês and the bull was reproduced 119 times, often countermarked with other smaller signets. Another official seal, representing a dolphin and club, appears 285 times. It is evident that the seals found in this deposit came from official documents preserved in the Temple archives.

the field. In Italy the coin-types of Neapolis[85] and Thurii[86] have been preserved on existing intaglios.

It is impossible to suppose that any private person could have made use of such well-known civic badges. Such gems were obviously executed solely for official purposes, and it is reasonable to infer that the same artists who executed the dies of the civic coinage were also employed to engrave these civic seals. When, therefore, we find Evænetos signing the dies associated with this fine design of Hêraklês strangling the lion we have every reason to infer, apart from the singular correspondence of the style and workmanship, that this artist was also the engraver of the signet gem presenting the same official type. The fact that it was found in the neighbourhood of Katanê, a scene of Evænetos' activity as a die-sinker, is certainly not inconsistent with this conclusion.

---

[85] In the British Museum ; and cf. Imhoof-Blumer und Keller, *op. cit.*, Taf. xxvi. 46.

[86] A perforated chalcedony gem in a private collection at Ruvo, in Apulia, of fine Greek workmanship, presents a most striking resemblance to the bull as it appears on Thurian tetradrachms of the first half of the Fourth Century, B.C.

PART VI

THE HISTORICAL OCCASIONS OF THE *DÂMARE-TEION* AND THE LATER "MEDALLIONS."

THE general conclusion derived from various lines of converging evidence, to which we have been led in the preceding Sections, that the earliest of the Syracusan "medallions" date back to the years immediately succeeding the approximate date of 415 B.C., leads us to an interesting point in our inquiry.

As long as it was believed, as it has been hitherto, that the first issue of these magnificent coins fell within the limits of the Dionysian Period, the precise historic occasion of this exceptional issue might remain in doubt.

Signor Cavallari, indeed, has recently put forward the suggestion[1] that the head on Kimôn's dekadrachms is that of the Nymph Kyanê, and that these coins record the defeat inflicted on the Carthaginians in 394 B.C. by Dionysios in the neighbourhood of her shrine, which had been chosen by him as his headquarters.

The mere fact, however, that the "medallions" of Kimôn, here specially referred to, were imitated on a series of Motyan types, some of them, at least, struck several years before the overthrow of that city by Dionysios in 397, is sufficient to exclude a reference to the

---

[1] In his account, published at Palermo, of the recently discovered shrine of Kyanê.

R

disaster that befell the Carthaginian host before Syracuse three years after that date. And when we are led back by a comparative study of the Syracusan and other types to seek the date of the first issue of these famous pieces, between the approximate dates 415—410 B.C., it becomes impossible not to connect them with the great historical event which marks that very period of years, the final overthrow, namely, of the Athenian invaders in 413 B.C., by sea on the waters of the Great Harbour, and by land in the gorge of the Assinaros.

That the crowning victory over the Athenians should have found a record on the Syracusan coin-types, at least in that indirect and allusive manner that was usual in the best days of Greek art, is rendered probable by more than one precedent. The abnormal size and value of these noble "medallions," warrants us in supposing that they were struck on some extraordinary occasion. But this presumption gains additional weight when it is remembered that coins of the same exceptional value of fifty silver litras had been struck two generations earlier, on the occasion of another crowning triumph of the Syracusan arms—the victory, namely, of Gelôn in alliance with Thêrôn of Akragas over the Carthaginian Hamilkar at Himera.

These coins, which derived their name of *Dâmareteia* from Gelôn's consort, require special consideration from their intimate connexion with our present subject, though the inquiry is involved in considerable difficulty from the fact that accounts differ as to their exact source and occasion.[2]

---

[2] For the Δαμαρέτειον, see especially Leake (*Trans. of R. Soc. of Lit.*, 2nd series, 1850, p. 283) and the monograph of F. Hultsch, *De Damareteo argenteo Syracusanorum Nummo*

According to the later grammarians, Hesychios,[3] and Pollux,[4] these memorial coins were struck out of the bullion derived from the jewellery which Dâmaretâ and other noble ladies of Syracuse had given up to provide the sinews of war at a moment when the treasury was exhausted through the struggle with Carthage. In this case the coins themselves, struck from gold jewellery in a moment of emergency, must have been of gold, and both Pollux and Hesychios imply that they were such. This statement, however, contains one radical error of fact, since the coins themselves—a few examples of which have come down to us—were undoubtedly of silver: indeed, no Syracusan gold coin seems to have been struck till about the time of the Athenian siege. Diodôros,[5] on the

---

(Dresden, 1862). Cf. too his *Gr. und röm. Metrologie* (2nd ed. Berlin, 1882, p. 433). The fact that the *Dâmareteion* must be sought in a silver coin was first pointed out by C. O. Müller, *Die Etrusker*, i. 397 (and cf. *Annali dell' Inst. di Corr. Arch*, 1830, p. 337); and the Duc de Luynes, *Ann. dell 'Inst* , &c. 1830, p. 81 *seqq.* (*Du Démarétion*), who first distinguished the true *Dâmareteion* of Gelôn's time from the later *Pentêkontalitra* of the Dionysian Period. Cf. Mommsen, *Röm. Münzwesen*, 79 (trad. Blacas I., 105) ; F. Lenormant, *Rev. Num.*, 1868, p. 9 *seqq.* ; Head, *Coinage of Syracuse*, p. 8. Böckh, *Staatshaushaltung der Athener* (3rd ed., p. 36), followed earlier writers in regarding the *Dâmareteion* as a gold coin.

[3] *S.v.* Δημαρέτιον. "Δημαρέτιον, νόμισμα ἐν Σικελίᾳ ὑπὸ Γέλωνος κοπὲν, ἐπιδούσης αὐτῷ Δημαρέτης τῆς γυναικὸς εἰς αὐτὸ τὸν κόσμον."

[4] *Onomasticon*, lib. ix. 85. "Ἡ Δημαρέτη Γέλωνος οὖσα γυνὴ, κατὰ τὸν πρὸς Λίβυας πόλεμον ἀποροῦντος αὐτοῦ, τὸν κόσμον αἰτησαμένη παρὰ τῶν γυναικῶν συγχωνεύσασα νόμισμα ἐκόψατο Δαμαρέτιον)." Pollux couples it with gold staters.

[5] Lib. xi. c. 26 :—" Στέφανον χρυσοῦν τῇ γυναικὶ τοῦ Γέλωνος Δαμαρέτῃ προσωμολόγησαν. αὕτη γὰρ ὑπ' αὐτῶν ἀξιωθεῖσα συνήργησε πλεῖστον εἰς τὴν σύνθεσιν τῆς εἰρήνης, καὶ στεφανωθεῖσα ὑπ' αὐτῶν ἑκατὸν ταλάντοις χρυσίου, νόμισμα ἐξέκοψε, τὸ κληθὲν ἀπ' ἐκείνης Δαμαρέτειον ˙ τοῦτο δ' εἶχεν Ἀττικὰς δραχμὰς δέκα, ἐκλήθη δὲ παρὰ τοῖς Σικελιώταις ἀπὸ τοῦ σταθμοῦ πεντηκοντάλιτρον."

other hand, describes the *Dâmareteia* as having been struck out of the money value of a hundred talents derived from the gold crown presented by the Carthaginians to Dâmaretâ in return for her good offices in securing them more favourable conditions of peace than they had otherwise expected. His additional statement that the coin "weighed[6] ten Attic drachmæ and was called a fifty-litra piece (πεντηκοντάλιτρον) by the Sicilian Greeks from its weight," shows that he rightly regarded it as a silver coin.

"Talent" is, unfortunately, almost always a vague denomination, but according to the generally accepted interpretation of the passage in Diodôros,[7] the hundred talents of gold mentioned as the value of the honorary crown, are taken to mean the small Attic talents of six gold drachmæ, or three staters, which, reckoning the proportion of gold to silver at that time as 13 to 1, would represent the equivalent of 7,800 silver drachmæ. In that case no more than 780 of these silver dekadrachms could have been struck, and even allowing for the great rarity of the pieces in question, this number must be regarded as too small for a special coinage which left such a mark in history.

It seems much more reasonable to suppose that the talents referred to by Diodôros were Sicilian gold talents

---

[6] For this force of ἔχειν = *to weigh*, see Hultsch, *op. cit.*, p. 13, who cites Thucydides (lib. ii., 13, 5), Diodôros himself (lib. ii., c. 9), and the usage of Greek metrological writers. He adds: "Diodorus igitur cum εἶχεν Ἀττικὰς δραχμὰς δέκα scripsit, nihil nisi pondus significare voluit: quasi vero animo præsensisset non defuturos esse qui minus recte id intellegerent addidit verba : ἐκλήθη δὲ παρὰ τοῖς Σικελιώταις ἀπὸ τοῦ σταθμοῦ πεντηκοντάλιτρον, quibus idem quod modo Attico pondere expresserit jam Siculorum pondere enuntiat."

[7] Cf. Hultsch, *Metrologie* (1882), p. 129 *seqq.*, and p. 433.

representing 120 gold litras, just as the Sicilian silver talent represented 120 litras of silver.[8] The wreath would thus furnish the more respectable sum of 2,400 gold drachmæ, answering in silver to 3,120 *pentēkontalitra.*

That the honorary crown sent by the Carthaginians to Dâmaretâ represented a substantial amount of bullion is made probable not only from the fact that silver sufficient for a special coinage was purchased from the gold that it produced, but from the analogy of other Punic crowns of the same class of which we have historic record. The gold crown, for example, offered by the Carthaginians in the temple of the Capitoline Jove in B.C. 341 (A.U.C. 413) weighed 25 lbs., or 1,875 Attic drachmæ.[9] Another, in the Temple of Jupiter in Tarraco, weighed 15 lbs. The crowns offered in later times by the Greek princes and cities to the Romans also afford a good parallel to the gift to Dâmaretâ, for their primary object was to give a graceful form to the presentation of a solid sum of money. Eumenês of Pergamos, for instance, sent the Romans a crown of " 15,000 gold drachmæ " (χρυσῶν).[10] Examples

---

[8] Hultsch (*De Damareteo*) assumes that the Sicilian gold talent would be simply the equivalent in gold of the silver talent. Taking, then, the proportionate value of gold to silver as 12 to 1, he arrives at the conclusion that the Sicilian gold talent (= 120 silver litras or 12 silver staters) was exactly the gold stater. But inasmuch as at a somewhat later period, when the Sicilian gold coinage begins, we find gold litras actually struck (cf. p. 63), it seems preferable to believe that 120 gold litras went to make up the gold talent. I observe that Leake (*Trans. of R. Soc. of Lit.*, 2nd Series, 1850, p. 356) had arrived at the same conclusion to which I had independently been led.

[9] Livy, vii., 38.

[10] Polybios, *Hist.* xxiv., 1, 7. More obscurity attaches to the contemporary wreath presented by the Ætolians to the Roman Consul at the time of their submission. Polybios (xxii. 13), after mentioning, a few paragraphs before, that 200 Euboic

like these seem more pertinent than the votive wreaths set
up in the Akropolis of Athens,[11] in which taste supplied a
larger ingredient than bullion, though even of one of these
we read that it weighed as much as 1,250 gold drachmæ.

The issue of this Dâmareteian coinage must be taken in
connexion with another contemporary act, the dedication,
namely, by Gelôn and his brothers, of a gold tripod to the
Delphian Apollo out of the Carthaginian spoils, according
to one account partly out of the Dâmareteian gold itself.

Diodôros, after recording the conclusion of peace with
the Carthaginians and the receipt by Dâmaretâ of the
golden crown of a hundred talents, in addition to the war
indemnity of two thousand talents, states that Gelôn
"built out of the spoils of war two splendid temples
dedicated to Dêmêtêr and Korê, and having made, with
sixteen talents, a votive tripod, set it up as a thank-offer-
ing in the Temenos of Apollo at Delphi."[12]   Simonidês of

---

talents were to be paid as indemnity, adds : " ἐδόθη δὲ αὐτῷ
καὶ στέφανος ἀπὸ ταλάντων πεντήκοντα καὶ ἑκατόν." This transaction appears in Livy (lib. xxviii., 9) : "Ambracienses coro-
nam auream Consuli centum et quinquaginta pondo," making the
weight of the wreath 150 lbs. This, reckoning 75 to the pound,
would represent 11,250 gold drachms, nearly a third less than the
gold wreath presented by Eumenês. But Livy seems to have
simply turned talents into pounds. According to Hultsch's
view these talents can only be the small goldsmiths' talents of
6 drachmæ. In this way the weight of the crown would be
reduced to 900 gold drachmæ—a paltry sum considering the
high standard of value set by contemporary usage on such
propitiatory gifts. Of the two versions, Livy's certainly seems
nearer the mark. A wreath of Ptolemy Philadelphos' time is
recorded to have weighed 10,000 gold staters.

[11] See Böckh. *Staatshaushaltung der Athener* (1886), i., p.
36 *seqq.* Many of the wreaths in the Akropolis weighed from
17½ to 100 drachms. Three gold wreaths dedicated to Athena
weighed respectively 245 drachms 1 obol., 272 dr. 3½ ob., and
232 dr. 5 ob.

[12] Diodôros, lib. xi. c. 26. "Ὁ Γέλων ἐκ μὲν τῶν λαφύρων

Keos,[13] on the other hand, in the epigram said to have been inscribed on the tripod itself, makes it speak as follows:—

"Φαμὶ Γέλων' Ἱέρωνα Πολύζηλον Θρασύβουλον
Παῖδας Δεινομένευς τὸν τρίποδ' ἀνθέμεναι
Ἐξ ἑκατὸν λιτρᾶν καὶ πεντήκοντα ταλάντων
Δαμαρετίου χρυσοῦ, τᾶς δεκάτας δεκάταν,
Βάρβαρα νικάσαντας ἔθνη, πολλὰν δὲ παρασχεῖν
Σύμμαχον Ἕλλασιν χεῖρ' ἐς ἐλευθερίαν."

However we are to account for the discrepancy of our two informants as to the number of talents devoted to the gold tripod, the most ordinary common-sense must refuse to believe that this splendid offering, celebrated alike by poet and historian, of the Syracusan *Stratêgos Autokratôr* and his brothers, weighed only 48 gold staters.[14] It is possible that Diodôros' 16 talents simply

---

κατεσκεύασε ναοὺς ἀξιολόγους Δήμητρος καὶ Κόρης, χρυσοῦν δὲ τρίποδα ποιήσας ἀπὸ ταλάντων ἑκκαίδεκα ἀνέθηκεν ἐς τὸ τέμενος τὸ ἐν Δελφοῖς Ἀπόλλωνι."

[13] Ep. cxcvi. Cf. Schol. ad Pind. *Pyth.* i., 155. Theopompos (Athen., vi., p. 231) mentions a gold Nikê, as well as a tripod, among the *Anathêmata* of Gelôn and Hierôn at Delphi. Dindorf, in his edition of Simonidês (Brunswick, 1835, p. 184), dismisses the lines commemorating the weight of the tripod with the remark: "Est hic iterum fetus grammaticuli doctrinam numariam incommode ostentantis." These lines, however, are as well authenticated as any in the epigram. They are given to the *Codex Palatinus* where the two last are omitted, and, are referred to by Suidas (*s.v.* Δαρείον, for Δαμαρετίον). Nor need the record of the value of the tripod, and the numismatic reference, at all surprise us when we find Simonidês, in another epigram (clx.), giving the amount of Parian drachms that went to the making of a small votive image of Artemis, and accompanying it with a reference to the coin-type of Paros:—

"'Αρτέμιδος τόδ' ἄγαλμα · διηκόσιοι γὰρ ὁ μισθός
Δραχμὰι ταὶ Πάριαι, τῶν ἐπίσημα τράγος."

[14] Yet such is Hultsch's conclusion in conformity with his view that the talents mentioned by Diodôros in the case of both wreath and tripod are the small goldsmith's talents of six

refer to Gelôn's contribution, and that the remaining 34 talents 100 litras represent the joint gift of the other three brothers. The total value of the tripod, according to the estimate of the Sicilian gold talent already given, would in that case be 1,220 gold drachmæ, amounting in weight to somewhat over 16 lbs.

That the tripod should be described as of Dâmareteian gold may perhaps be taken as a poetic licence, yet it serves to indicate the close connexion existing in men's minds between the votive *anathéma* set up in the Delphic shrine of Apollo and the new commemorative coinage. Both the coins and the tripod were derived from the gifts or spoils of the vanquished; both alike were regarded as tokens of victory, and the coins themselves have preserved a symbol of dedication that makes it in the highest degree probable that they too, like the tripod, were in the first instance designed as offerings of thanksgiving—χαριστήρια—to the same God, in the one case to be devoted to his Delphian sanctuary, in the other, we may well believe, to the service of a local Syracusan festival in his honour. Upon the reverse of the Dâmareteion, beneath the usual agonistic type of the quadriga, is seen a couchant lion, the symbolic animal of Apollo, precisely as it appears associated with his head on contemporary coins of Leontini.[15] That the issue of these coins connected itself

---

gold drachms. He endeavours to reconcile Diodôros' account with that of Simonidês by supposing that the latter refers to a Sicilian gold talent equal to the silver talent of 120 litras. This talent, according to his view, taking the relation of gold to silver as 12 to 1, amounted to one gold stater. Fifty talents and 100 litras would thus represent 101 Attic drachms, which would approximate to the 96 Attic drachms deduced by him from the 16 talents of Diodôros.

[15] Cf. Head, *Historia Numorum*, p. 152.

with the celebration of games in Apollo's honour must
be regarded therefore as unquestionable. From the great
rarity of these early fifty-litra pieces we are tempted
even to go a step farther, and to venture the suggestion
that the coins themselves were in the first instance
dedicated to the local shrine of Apollo, and that they
may have served, like the Metapontine silver staters with
the inscription Aχελοιο αεθλον,[16] as actual prizes in a
contest held in his honour.

Fig. 9.—The "Dâmareteion."

The specially commemorative character of this first
"medallion" issue at Syracuse is of first-rate importance
in its relation to the revival in the years immediately
succeeding the Athenian siege of a fresh issue of the
same denomination. But it is easy to cite other parallels
which justify us in considering that such an event as
the annihilation of the Athenian *Armada* would not be
left uncommemorated on the Syracusan dies. Thus, for
instance, the *Pistrix* beneath the chariot on certain coins
of Hierôn I., with the allusion that it conveys to Poseidôn,
has been reasonably taken to symbolize the great sea

---

[16] See below, p. 134.

s

victory over the Etruscans off Kymê in 474 B.C.,[17] once more, no doubt, in connexion with special hippic contests in honour of the God. The games instituted by Pyrrhos after the capture of Eryx as a tribute of devotion to Hêraklês, the legendary slayer of its eponymous giant, seem to have left their mark on his Syracusan bronze pieces. At a slightly earlier date the victory of Agathoklês over the Carthaginians in Africa was commemorated both in his gold and silver coinage; in the former case under the guise of a tribute to Athênê,[18] in the latter case to Korê. The trophy of arms raised by Nikê on the reverse of the Agathokleian tetradrachm, in which the reference to the consecrated spoils of war is undoubted, recalls the arms exhibited on the steps beneath the victorious chariot on the dekadrachm types before us. And if, in the latter trophy, a Carthaginian characteristic has been detected in the conical form of the helmet,[19] the shield and helmet on our medallions show a marked resemblance to those of the prostrate warrior on the fine didrachm of Gela, which, according to Holm's ingenious hypothesis, commemorated the assistance rendered by the Gelôan cavalry to the Syracusans in their struggle with the Athenians.[20]

---

[17] Head, *Coins of Syracuse*, p. 9.

[18] Head, *Historia Numorum*, p. 159; cf. Diod. xxii. 11.

[19] Gardner, *Types of Greek Coins*, p. 184. "Victory is nailing to the frame a conical helmet in shape like that 'Tyrrhenian' helmet dedicated to Zeus by Hiero I." (See *B. M. Guide to Bronze Room*, p. 12.)

[20] Cited in Schubring. *Die Münzen von Gela; Berliner Blätter*, vi. p. 148. The engraver of this Gelan coin has been careful to indicate the difference between the helmet of the horseman, which is of a Phrygian character, and that of the prostrate enemy, which is provided with ear-pieces and a long crest like those in the exergue of the Syracusan dekadrachms. The shield is of absolutely the same shape.

That the revived issue of the Syracusan fifty-litra pieces, answering in their denomination to the earlier Dâmareteia, connects itself with the Syracusan triumph over the Athenians, is made the more probable by the appearance on some tetradrachms struck about the same date of an undoubted reference to the spoils of a naval victory. In the fine reverse design of certain tetradrachms from the hands of the artist Evarchidas, a variety of which occurred in the Santa Maria hoard, Professor Salinas has already recognised[21] an allusion to the defeat of the Athenian fleet in the Great Harbour of Syracuse, whether that of the beginning or of the autumn of 413 it might be difficult to determine. The obverse of this type displays a female head apparently representing Arethusa, and signed by the artist Phrygillos on the ampyx of her sphendonê. Upon the reverse Persephonê appears guiding with her left hand the reins of her galloping steeds, and in the other holding aloft a flaming torch in place of the usual goad of the charioteer, while Nikê, who flies forward to greet her, holds in her left hand the ἄφλαστον, or aplustre, the ornament of the poop of one of the captured vessels. The appearance of the Chthonic Goddess on this piece and the manner in which Nikê holds the naval trophy towards the burning torch may, perhaps, suggest a reference to a wholesale devotion of the spoils of war by fire to the deities of the Nether World, to which we find more than one reference in ancient writers.

Comparing these pieces that commemorate the naval victory with the dekadrachm types, we are struck with

---

[21] *Notizie degli Scavi*, 1888, p. 15 *seqq*. Examples of these types are also given in my article on *New Artists' Signatures on Sicilian Coins*, Pl. X., 6, 7, of the present volume.

certain points of correspondence which can hardly be the result of accident. Here, too, we see alternately Persephonê and Arethusa taking the place of honour on the die. Here, too, on the reverse, beside the agonistic part of the design, is seen a trophy, this time of arms, and appropriate to victory on land. And if in the former case there seems good reason to connect the *aplustre* offered to the Nether Goddess with the maritime discomfiture of the Athenians, we are tempted to connect the consecrated prize of arms, symbolizing the guerdon of a contest held in the honour of a God, with that supreme triumph on the land side which consigned the remnant of the Athenian army to the quarries of Achradina.

The fact that the earlier *Dámareteia* were coined out of the money produced by a gold wreath, which, though presented to Gelôn's consort, was treated as being practically part of the spoils of war, and that they were probably partly supplied by the actual loot or indemnity, strongly favours the suggestion that the revived issue of these *pentêkontalitra* may have been derived from a similar source.

We have, indeed, some historic warrant for believing that the "medallions" now struck were coined out of the silver poured into the Syracusan treasury by the successful issue of the war. There can be no doubt that, both by actual booty and the subsequent ransom of prisoners, a large amount of silver bullion fell into the hands of the Syracusans at the time of the Athenian overthrow. A very considerable sum of money was actually taken on the Athenian prisoners. Thus, Thucydides tells us that on the surrender of the 6,000 survivors of Demosthenes' division, four shields were filled with the silver money that

they carried on their persons.[22]   But the forces of the
retreating Athenians were estimated by the historian at
40,000, and assuming that even half of these were despoiled
in the same manner by their conquerors, the total number
of shields-full collected may well have exceeded a dozen.
If we may judge from the capacity of the shields represented on the coins themselves, the cavities of which may
be estimated at $2\frac{1}{2}$ feet in breadth, and nearly a foot in
central depth, the silver bullion obtained from this source
alone must have amounted to a very considerable sum.
From Thucydides' statement we may, perhaps, form
the deduction that, for purposes of general security as
well as of individual aid in a hazardous retreat, a large
part of the military chest had been divided amongst the
rank and file.

It is probable that a large part at least of this prize
silver was actually consecrated, with the arms, to one or
more tutelary divinities, and that it therefore could not be
used for the ordinary purposes of the mint.   But the
existence of such a Sacred Fund would make it easy to
understand how, on the institution of new games, such as
followed the victory over the Athenians, an extraordinary
coinage might be issued, having a special honorific func-
tion, in connexion with them.

According to this view the earlier, at least, of these fine
pieces, inscribed **ΑΘΛΑ**, may have been coined of prize
silver, and themselves, in part, have served to reward the
winners in the games.   In the case of many of these coins,
however, this limitation cannot be considered tenable. The
comparative abundance of the ordinary dekadrachm types,   ˙

---

[22] Thuc., lib. vii. 82.   " Καὶ τὸ ἀργύριον ὃ εἶχον ἅπαν κατέθεσαν
ἐσβαλόντες ἐς ἀσπίδας ὑπτίας, καὶ ἐνέπλησαν ἀσπίδας τέσσαρας."

and notably the prolific coinage of Evænetos, forbids us to regard them as having been exclusively devoted to the rewarding of the winners; and even if we extend their application to other expenses connected with the games, it will hardly sufficiently account for their wide-spread use. So much, however, it seems legitimate to infer from the character of the types, as well as from analogous usage, that their dates of issue corresponded with those of the periodic, perhaps annual, games. On the other hand, this does not exclude the possibility that some of the scarcer and more exceptional types may have been designed for more purely agonistic purposes. That the wreath and arms should have been here supplemented by a prize in money is in accordance with numerous analogies. We know that at Athens as much as five hundred drachmæ was given to citizens who returned victorious from the Olympic festival. In the military games at Keos, again, as already noticed, a prize of silver drachmæ was added to the prize of arms,[23] and there is evidence that in the case of local games, where such prize payments were constantly recurring, a special coinage was occasionally issued, no doubt from some temple treasury, to supply a type of money appropriate to the occasion. Of such, in early times, a memorable example is found in the Metapontine didrachms bearing the inscription, in archaic orthography, Αχελοιο αεθλον, and which doubtless celebrate the prize of a contest held on the banks of the Bradanos in honour of the Father of all Greek Rivers. In later times, as may be gathered both from inscriptions and from the types of several autonomous coins of Asia Minor, struck under the Roman Empire, this practice had gained a wide extension; these local coinages,

---

[23] C. I. G., ii. 2360.

however, no doubt covering other expenses and necessities
of commerce created by the festival, besides the actual
payment to the winner.

It has, indeed, already been suggested by Eckhel[24] that
the Syracusan dekadrachms inscribed AΘΛA, may have
been struck as prize-money either for the purpose of
rewarding victors in the games or in actual warfare, and
that the inscription may therefore refer to the coin itself.
The idea that they may represent the material reward
of winners in the games has also commended itself to
Hultsch.[25] The great rarity of what must be regarded
as the earliest of these dekadrachm types, the coins,
namely, engraved by Kimôn, with the head of Arethusa
in low relief, is possibly to be explained on this hypothesis,
while the fact that the newly-discovered type exists only
in a single example points yet more strongly to this conclusion. In the case, again, of this unique medallion by
the New Artist, the inscription AΘΛA on the reverse
appears in letters of double the size and prominence of
the ⵉYPAKOⵉIΩN on the obverse, and certainly looks
as if it referred to the coin itself as an integral part of a
sum of prize-money, quite as much as to the panoply
represented below. The solitary occurrence of this type
may also be explained on the hypothesis that it was
specially coined to serve in a more exclusive sense than
the ordinary dekadrachms, as part of the actual AΘΛA of
a winner in a local ἀγὼν ἀργυρίτης. A limited issue of
the same kind may further account for the fact that of
the Akragantine dekadrachms only four specimens are
known.

---

[24] *Doctrina Numorum,* i., p. xviii.; cf. p. 243. Eckhel is
followed by Böckh, *Metrologische Untersuchungen,* p. 320.

[25] *De Damareteo,* &c., p. 27.

In the case of these latter coins, moreover, there is an epigraphic feature which may even turn out to stamp them as belonging to the same class of **AⵔΛΑ** as the Syracusan example. This is the appearance immediately behind, and, indeed, almost in contiguity with, the head of the charioteer on the reverse of a large **A**,[26] the purport of which has hitherto · perplexed numismatists. By Von Sallet, Weil, and others, it has been taken to represent an artist's signature ; but the position in which it occurs, and its solitary prominence in this position, does not by any means correspond to the usual methods and locations of signature amongst contemporary Sicilian engravers.[27] Its very distinct connexion with the charioteer has, indeed, been lately used as an argument by Dr. Kinch[28] in favour of his theory that all the signatures that at this time appear, refer not to the engravers of the dies, but to actual winners in the games. Dr. Kinch has failed to see the one unanswerable objection to his line of argument, namely, that the signature follows the style of engraving, and that · whether, for instance, the name of Evænetos appears at Syracuse, at Kamarina, or at Katanê, it is always associated with the same individualities of handiwork. But the

---

[26] See esp. Weil, *Künstlerinschriften*, &c., p. 13. All the known examples according to Weil are from the same reverse die. In Salinas' engraving (*Le Monete delle Antiche Città di Sicilia*, Tav. viii. 5, 6), the **A** is not reproduced.

[27] All reverse signatures on Sicilian coins are either immediately above, upon, or below the exergual line, or in a tablet held by Victory. On the larger coins, with the exception of the doubtful instances of Hêrakleidas, there do not seem to be any single-letter signatures of artists even in this position. On the obverse the initial letter of Proklês appears in one instance on a Katanæan didrachm.

[28] *Observations sur les noms attribués aux Graveurs des Monnaies grecques* (*Revue Numismatique*, 1889, p. 473 *seqq.*).

solitary **A** on this Akragantine coin belongs, as already remarked, to a different category from such authenticated artists' signatures as those of Evænetos and his fellows, and there is in this instance this element of truth in Dr. Kinch's suggestion, that the inscribed letter is apparently intended to stand in very close relation to the winner of the chariot race. As a matter of fact, this solitary **A** appears as a stamp, the significance of which must have had a general acceptation, on a whole series of Sicilian coins struck about this period, but in nowise allied in point of style. Amongst the hundred-litra gold pieces of Syracuse already referred to,[29] with the head of Arethusa and Hêraklês strangling the lion, struck contemporaneously with the silver pentékontalitra of Evænetos and Kimôn, and exhibiting in more or less abbreviated forms the names of both artists, the recent find at Avola, near Noto, has brought to light a variety, in which a conspicuous sideways-slanting **A** is introduced beneath the upright **K**, that here, no doubt, stands for Kimôn's signature.[30] On a drachm of Katania an **A** appears stamped sideways on the neck of a youthful head, perhaps of the local River-God Amenanos.[31] On two fine tetradrachms of Syracuse, again, belonging to the period which immediately precedes the appearance of recognised artists' signatures, an **A** is seen stamped in one instance on the upper part of the sakkos-covered head,[32] in the other case on the

---

[29] See p. 93.

[30] On other examples, **KI** is found. See p. 94.

[31] A. Löbbecke, *Zeitschr. f. Numismatik*, 1887, p. 36, and Taf. iii. 1. The head is there described as Apollo's, but the *tænia* in place of laurel-wreath and the style of hair seem better to answer to the local types with the head of Amenanos.

[32] Kinch, *loc. cit.*, p. 409. In the Copenhagen Museum.

neck of the Nymph or Goddess just below the earring,[33] while on a third coin[34] it is seen on the front of the chariot on the reverse, a position which recalls the contiguity to the Akragantine charioteer. Finally, on some varieties of a late tetradrachm of Selinûs a large A appears in incuse upon the base that supports the statue of the bull.[35] It is, perhaps, a fair conjecture that in all these cases the A thus anomalously and conspicuously introduced represents the stamp of consecration for a special religious purpose, and the marked association of it with the charioteer on the Akragantine coin with the chariot on the Syracusan, makes it probable that this purpose was not unconnected with the games. It is even possible, though this is by no means a necessary explanation, that the A here is explained by the fuller legend $\alpha\epsilon\theta\lambda o\nu$ of the Metapontine coin in the signification of prize money.

In any case, the number of early Greek types which were originally coined for a definite religious object, and only in a secondary way became part of the ordinary currency, is probably more considerable than has been hitherto supposed.

The armour exhibited in the exergual space of our "medallions," consisting of shield, greaves, breast-plate and helmet, makes up together the $\pi\alpha\nu o\pi\lambda\acute{\iota}\alpha$, or full hoplite accoutrement, such as in the Greek cities was the recognised prize of military valour.[36] The martial charac-

---

[33] *B. M. Cat.*, *Syracuse*, 116. I have a fine example in my own collection found near Catania. Kinch interprets this design as showing that the winner, A, consecrates an earring (in the other case a *sphendonê*) to the divinity

[34] *B. M. Cat.*, *Syracuse*, No. 109.

[35] A specimen of this coin is in my own collection.

[36] Thus Isokrates says of his father (*De Bigis*, § 29): "Καὶ . . . ὅτε Φορμίων ἐξήγαγεν ἐπὶ Θράκης χιλίους Ἀθηναίων ὁπλίτας

ter of this prize is certainly significant; there can be no
doubt, however, that in the present instance this panoply
appears immediately, at least, in an agonistic connexion,
and we may thus gather that the contest referred to was
of the kind known as ἀγών ἀθλοφόρος, in which the
prizes had a material value. It is, therefore, impossible
in this case, as in some other Sicilian coin types, to trace
an allusion to the Olympian games, where the wild olive
wreath was the only tangible reward. The heroic practice,
such as it is recorded for us by Homer[37] in his account of
the contests in honour of Patroklos, of offering tripods,
cauldrons, and other objects of value, including arms, to
the winners,[38] does not seem to have been adhered to at
any of the four great Games of Greece. The returning
winner was, indeed, often presented, as at Athens, for
instance, with pecuniary and other material rewards by
his gratified fellow-citizens, but this is another matter;
and on the other hand, in some of the less celebrated contests, prizes of value, such as silver cups and bronze
vessels, were not infrequently awarded. It would, however, appear that the only recorded festivals at which
arms were given as prizes were the Hekatombœa at
Argos, in which a shield was presented to the victor in

ἐπιλεξάμενος τοὺς ἀρίστους, μετὰ τούτων στρατευσάμενος τοιοῦτος
ἦν ἐν τοῖς κινδύνοις ὥστε στεφανωθῆναι καὶ πανοπλίαν λαβεῖν παρὰ
τοῦ στρατηγοῦ." Cf. Eckhel, *Doctrina Numorum* (i. p. 243),
and Hulsch, *De Damareteo argenteo Syracusanorum Nummo*,
Dresden, 1862, p. 25. The spear, however, is not indicated in
the "medallions."

[37] Il. Ψ 251.

[38] So too Virgil, *Æn.* v. 106—112:

> " *Munera principio ante oculos circoque locantur*
> *In medio ; sacri tripodes, viridesque coronæ*
> *Et palmæ, pretium victoribus, armaque et ostro*
> *Perfusæ vestes, argenti aurique talenta.*"

addition to the myrtle wreath, and the military games in Keos, in which the guerdon consisted of arms and silver drachmæ.[39] We must, therefore, look to some local festival to explain the introduction of this new and martial reward at Syracuse.

As a matter of fact, some of the local games instituted by the Sikeliote Greeks had, at a considerably earlier date, attained sufficient celebrity to attract even competitors from the Mother-Country.[40] Hierôn of Syracuse had founded Nemean games at his Ætna, at which, as we learn from Pindar,[41] the Corinthian Xenophôn had gained a victory. At Syracuse itself, Isthmian games had been founded in imitation of her Mother-City, in which also the same Corinthian citizen had successfully competed. On the occasion again of the banishment of Thrasybulos in 446 B.C., and the establishment of a democratic government at Syracuse, yearly games had been introduced with great splendour, under the name of "Eleutheria," in honour of Zeus Eleutherios, to whom at the same time a colossal statue was set up.[42]

---

[39] See G. Humbert, art. "Certamen," in Daremberg et Saglio, *Dict. des Antiquités.*

[40] Cf. Freeman, *Sicily*, ii., p. 268 and Note xxv. p. 531 (*Local Sikeliot Games*).

[41] *Ol.* xiii., 111 or 156 :—

"Ταί θ' ὑπ' Αἴτνας ὑψιλόφου καλλίπλουτοι
πόλιες."

According to one Scholiast : "πόλεις δὲ λέγει τὰς Συρακούσας. . . . Ἴσθμια γὰρ καὶ ἐν αὐταῖς τελεῖται"; while another says of Ætna : "ἐκεῖ γὰρ ἄγεται ἀγών Νέμεα καλούμενος."

[42] Diod., lib. xi., c. 72 : "Καταλύσαντες τὴν Θρασυβούλου τυραννίδα, συνήγαγον ἐκκλησίαν καὶ περὶ τῆς ἰδίας δημοκρατίας βουλευσάμενοι πάντες ὁμογνωμόνως ἐψηφίσαντο Διὸς μὲν ἐλευθερίου κολοττιαῖον ἀνδρίαντα κατασκευάσαι, κατ' ἐνιαυτὸν δὲ θύειν 'Ελευθέρια καὶ ἀγῶνας ἐπιφανεῖς ποιεῖν κατὰ τὴν αὐτὴν ἡμέραν ἐν ᾗ τὸν τύραννον καταλύσαντες ἠλευθέρωσαν τὴν πατρίδα."

But the prizes exhibited on our "medallions" assuredly connect themselves with an agonistic festival of more recent foundation at Syracuse than either the Nemea, Isthmia, or Eleutheria. The evidence which points to the times immediately succeeding the Athenians' defeat as the date of the first issue of these revived *Dâmareteia*, gives us good warrant for connecting this exceptional coinage with the New Games then instituted to commemorate the event, and which from the fatal stream whose gorge was the scene of the supreme overthrow were known as the *Assinaria*.[43]

In the case of the tetradrachms already cited, Persephonè herself, in the guise of a winner of the chariot race, receives at once the wreath of victory and the trophy of the captured vessels. In the other instance the spoils of the Athenian hoplites seem to have actually served as the winner's prize. But it is probable that even in this instance the armour on the coin is to be considered as the consecrated guerdon of a tutelary divinity of the city, and as rather typifying than actually representing the prize of a mere mortal winner at the games. The arms which before all others a Syracusan must have had in his mind were the *spolia opima* of Nikias himself, an elaborately wrought shield attributed to whom was shown at a much later date, as Plutarch informs us, suspended in one of their temples.[44] Plutarch's description of the surface of this shield as " a web-work of gold and purple welded together in a certain fashion," is suggestive of the

---

[43] Plutarch, *Nikias*, c. xxviii., 1.

[44] Plutarch. *Nikias*, c. xxviii., 4. " Πυνθάνομαι δὲ μέχρι νῦν ἐν Συρακούσαις ἀσπίδα πρὸς ἱερῷ δείκνυσθαι, Νικίου μὲν λεγομένην, χρυσοῦ δὲ καὶ πορφύρας ἕν πως πρὸς ἄλληλα μεμιγμένους δι᾽ ὑφῆς συγκεκροτημένην."

enamelled ornamentation on " Late Celtic," shields which
may, as in so many analogous instances, represent a Greek
tradition. It has been already noticed that the boss of the
shield on the dekadrachm of the New Artist from the Santa
Maria hoard shows traces of having been surrounded with
an ornamental zone, a detail quite in keeping with the
elaborate decoration which a minute study reveals upon
the greaves, cuirass, and helmet of the same trophy.

It is then in connexion with the institution of the New
Assinarian Games commemorating the Athenian overthrow that, after an interval of over two generations, the
noble fifty-litra pieces were once more issued by the
Syracusan mint. Their earlier appearance under the form
of the *Dâmareteia* had been due to the signal triumph of
Gelôn and his allies over the Carthaginians in the great
day of Himera ; and the lion symbol that these display
betokens, as we have seen, that they were in all probability
the guerdon of local Games in honour of Apollo. In
the present case the trophy of arms in the exergue of the
"medallions" may be held to have a special appropriateness to the River-God Assinaros, in whose honour the
New Games were instituted. Plutarch in fact informs
us[45] that on the occasion of the great victory the finest and
tallest trees along the banks of the stream were hung with
the panoplies of arms taken from the captive Athenians.

In the case of the *Dâmareteia* the female head on the
obverse side shows, however, that the local Goddess or
Nymph whose effigy had from the earliest times been a
constant feature of the Syracusan coin-types claimed her
share of the monetary tribute with the divine patron of the

---

[45] *Nikias*, c. xxvii. 8 : " τοὺς, δὲ φανερῶς ἐαλωκότας ἀθροίσαντες
τὰ μὲν κάλλιστα καὶ μέγιστα δένδρα τῶν περὶ τὸν ποταμὸν ἀνέθησαν
αἰχμαλώτοις πανοπλίαις."

Games. And so too, in the case of the revived issue of
the *pentékontalitra*, though the prize arms and chariot on
the reverse may, as suggested, connect themselves with
the River-God in whose honour the New Games were
instituted after the Athenian overthrow beside his waters,
the obverse types still commemorate the archaic cult of
the Goddess of the Nether World and the Nymph whose
miraculous fountain welled forth in the island citadel of
Syracuse. The association of Arethusa, who had watched
the destruction of the Athenian fleet, is certainly appropriate, nor less so the tribute to Persephonê on the
"medallion" types of the New Artist and Evænetos. As
a Chthonic Goddess, the consort of Aidoneus, the daughter
of Dêmêtêr Erinnys, whose shrine with that of her Mother
had looked down on some of the most stirring scenes of
that long struggle, she had certainly some claim to share
the spoils and honours of the crowning victory.

The Assinarian Games, as we further learn from Plutarch,[46] were first celebrated in September, 412, on the
first anniversary of the victory, and it is to this date that
the first distribution of these noble pieces must in all
probability be referred.

---

[46] Plutarch, *Nik.* xxviii., "ἡμέρα δ' ἦν τετρὰς φθίνοντος τοῦ
Καρνείου μηνός, ὃν Ἀθηναῖοι Μεταγειτνιῶνα προσαγορεύουσι."
Mr. Freeman, following Holm, fixes the day as September 18,
412. The engraving of the dies may have been put in hand
shortly after the victory itself, in the autumn, namely, of
413 B.C.

Part VII

CHRONOLOGICAL CONCLUSIONS BEARING ON THE SYRACUSAN COINAGE.

THE chronological results arrived at in the foregoing Sections, not only with regard to the first issue of the Syracusan "medallions" but to that of a large number of related pieces of other denominations, show that the hitherto accepted views as to the date of the Syracusan coin-types of the last decades of the Fifth and the first half of the Fourth Century B.C. need considerable revision.

It has been shown that the early tetradrachm type of Evænetos dates back in all probability to about 425 B.C., and that the still earlier signed work of Eumenês with the signature EVMH NOV, and of Sôsiôn, must therefore be thrown back some ten or fifteen years earlier than this. It has been further shown that what may be called the "Period of the Coiled Earring" comes to a close about the date of the Athenian siege, and that the works of the later group of engravers, Eukleidas, Euth . . ., Phrygillos and Evarchidas, as well as all those executed in Evænetos' earlier "manner," belong in the main to the Period 425—413 B.C.

With the Athenian overthrow of 413 and the newly instituted Games begins the revived issue of the silver *pentékontalitra*, Kimôn's earlier types taking precedence. In close relation to the head of Arethusa as she appears

on Kimôn's early " Medallions " stand the tetradrachm
types signed by Parme . . . (Pl. I. Fig. 6), together
with some allied pieces (Pl. I. Fig. 7)[1], and though the
forms of earrings point to a somewhat later date there
seems no sufficient reason for bringing down the issue of
these types more than a decade beyond that of the first
" medallions." On the other hand Kimôn's tetradrachms
with the profile head of the Nymph in every way correspond with his second dekadrachm type[2] struck about
410 B.C., while there is conclusive evidence that his facing
head of Arethusa had already appeared before the close
of B.C. 409, when it was copied at Himera.

The parallelism with this latter coin both in style and
design presented by Eukleidas' tetradrachm, with the
facing head of Pallas,[3] tends, as we have seen, to show
that this coin was issued at least as early as Kimôn's
masterpiece. This chronological equation is corrobo-
rated, moreover, as already noticed, by the fact that an
example of Eukleidas' coin occurred in the great Naxos
hoard deposited, as I hope to show,[4] at the latest by
410 B.C.

This conclusion further enables us to establish the approximate date of two other important types for which the
same reverse die was used as that which accompanies
Eukleidas' facing head of Pallas. One of these is the
tetradrachm exhibiting on the obverse the exquisite design
of the Korê with the ear of barley shooting up above her
forehead and her long tresses falling about her neck,[5] and
it is to be observed that the earring that she wears is of

---

[1] See p. 58.   [2] See p. 57.
[3] Head, *op. cit.*, Pl. IV., 10.   Cf. p. 72.
[4] See Appendix B.
[5] Head, *Coins of Syracuse*, Pl. V., 4.

the old-fashioned coiled type. The other coin[6] associated
with this Eukleidian die, an example of which occurred
in the Santa Maria hoard, also shows a very beautiful
female head, the full artistic significance of which seems
hitherto to have escaped notice and may therefore call for
a few words. A representation of this type from a specimen in the British Museum is given below, Fig. 10. The
features, for purity of outline, are unsurpassed in the
Syracusan series. The hair is bound up into a kind of
top-knot behind resembling that of the flying Nikê on the
reverse of one of Evænetos' "medallions" (Pl. V. fig.

Fig. 10.—SYRACUSAN TETRADRACHM, WITH HEAD OF NIKÊ.

10), and otherwise akin to some earlier Syracusan types of
the late Transitional Period.[7] The earring is of a remarkable form, and as such marks the period of varied fashions
in the use of this ornament which intervened between that
characterized by the fixed use of the coil-earring and that
of the triple pendant. It will be seen, that as this coin
has been hitherto represented,[8] the earring slopes forwards
in a curious way as if in defiance of the laws of gravity.
But in truth the earring is as it were the needle of the
compass which gives the true bearing of the whole design.

---

[6] Op. cit., Pl. V., 5.   [7] Head, op. cit., Pl. II., figs. 12, 13.
[8] Castelli, Sic. Vet. Num.; Auct. i., Tab. vii., 3; Head, Coins
of Syracuse, Pl. V., 5.

It is the head and not the pendent ornament that is intended to bend forward, and this head with the waving top-knot like that of the Victory on the "medallion," is the head of a flying Nikê.[9] The earring in fact enables us to supply the wings.

One other tetradrachm type of the same period seems to call for special mention. This is the fine coin presenting on the obverse a female head with somewhat flowing hair associated with the signature IM. From its remarkable style and from the device of the lion tearing down the bull on the exergue of the reverse, so strongly suggestive of the coin-types of Akanthos and Asia, this piece has been by Mr. Poole[10] attributed to an Ionian artist. The full rounded form of the chin as here shown is strongly suggestive of the Arethusa on Kimôn's earliest dekadrachm type, and the flowing tresses have a certain affinity with those of the Korê as designed by the New Artist. There can, in any case, be little doubt as to the pre-Dionysian da'e of this type. The earring seems to be of the earlier coiled form. The inscription is retrograde and shows the early N, and the quadriga scheme connects this tetradrachm with a more or less contemporary group of coins, including those by Kimôn and Eukleidas with

---

[9] This throws a retrospective light on the similar heads of the Transitional Period, and another of a date more nearly approaching the present example, though in these cases the head is not bowed forwards. The Winged Nikê appears with a similar top-knot on coins of Terina.

[10] *Num. Chron.*, 1864, p. 247 ("On Greek Coins as Illustrating Greek Art"). Mr. Head (*Coins of Syracuse*, p. 22) remarks on this type: "Whether the peculiar style of this piece, so different from the other tetradrachms of Syracuse, is due to its being the work of a native of Greece proper or Asia Minor, or only to its being ten or twenty years later, it is impossible to say."

the facing heads of Arethusa and Pallas, some of which are certainly anterior to 409 B.C.[11]

It will be seen that, according to this classification, all the Syracusan tetradrachms belonging to the period of the signed coinage fall into one or other of the above groups. In other words they are all anterior to the beginning of the Fourth Century within the limits of which the bulk of them have been hitherto included. As already pointed out, the presence of the later letters Ω and H on many of these coins cannot be regarded as an argument against their comparatively early date, for we find the new letters already on the earliest work of Sôsiôn and Eumenês, which on general grounds may be referred to the approximate date 440 B.C., about which time the Ω also makes its appearance at Thurii and Kaulonia in Italy. At Tarentum, indeed, it is found at least as early as 450 B.C. On the other hand, speaking generally, the whole of the signed tetradrachms of Syracuse and the other pieces contemporary with them still belong to what may be called the period of transitional epigraphy. On a gold hundred-litra piece of Kimôn, struck about the same time as his tetradrachms, the form ϚYPAKOϚION is still found, and Phrygillos, Euth . . ., Evarchidas, Eukleidas, and Evænetos, on his early dies, still associated their signatures with coins that display transitional traits in the orthography of the civic legend.

The approximate chronological results as regards the Syracusan coinage arrived at in the course of the present study may be tabulated as follows :—

---

[11] An obverse by IM . . . is found on a drachm (B. M. Cat , Syracuse, 233), associated with a reverse signed by Kimôn.

B.C.

Early signed tetradrachms by Sósión and
  Eumenês [" **EVMHⱮOV** "] . . . . *c.* 440

[*Ω and* **H** *employed in signatures: new letter-*
  forms used with uncertain force.]

Later coins of Eumenês [" **EYMENOY** "] . *c.* 430—415

Early tetradrachm of Evænetos [**EYAINETO**
  on tablet] . .. . *c.* 425

Other types in Evænetos' "early manner";
  coins by Euth . . . , Phrygillos, Evar-
  chidas, Eukleidas, etc., and other contem-
  porary pieces with coiled earrings and
  transitional epigraphy . . . *c.* 425—413

FINAL DEFEAT OF THE ATHENIANS AND IN-
  STITUTION OF THE "*ASSINARIAN GAMES*" . 413

ASSINARIAN GAMES FIRST CELEBRATED, SEPT. 13 . 412

REISSUE OF SILVER PENTÊKONTALITRA.

  [Variant forms of earring come into use
    about this epoch.]

Kimôn's " Medallion " Type I. 412

Kimôn's " Medallion " Type II., and similar
  tetradrachm . . . . . . *c.* 410

" CARTHAGINIAN " COINAGE AT MOTYA AND
  PANORMOS. KIMÔN'S " MEDALLION "
  TYPES I. AND II. IMITATED . . *c.* 410—408

Kimôn's tetradrachm with facing head of
  Arethusa . . . . *c.* 409

  [Imitated at Himera, destroyed at close of B.C. 409.]

Tetradrachm types by Parme . . . , Im . . , etc. c. 413—405

SYRACUSAN GOLD HUNDRED- AND FIFTY-
  LITRA PIECES FIRST ISSUED . . . . *c.* 408

FIRST ISSUE OF CARTHAGINIAN CAMP PIECES
  WITH HORSE AND HALF HORSE IMITATED
  FROM GOLD COINS OF SYRACUSE AND GELA *c.* 406—405

TYRANNY OF DIONYSIOS I. BEGINS . . . 406

The conclusion to which we have thus been led, that all the tetradrachm types struck at Syracuse during the finest period of art belong to a date anterior to 400 B.C., will appear to some revolutionary. And undoubtedly it raises great difficulties. But on the other hand, the present system of chronology, as applied to these Syracusan coin-types, raises questions which it seems even more difficult to answer.

How, it may well be asked, if the majority of these tetradrachm types belong to the Dionysian Period, does it happen that tetradrachms in Evænetos' later style, as exhibited by his "medallions," are absolutely unknown?

How is it, moreover, that whereas tetradrachms of Kimôn, reproducing the earlier "medallion" head, Type II., struck from about 410 B.C., are known, his commoner dekadrachms, Type III., which were first abundantly struck in the last two or three years of the Fifth Century find no counterpart amongst his tetradrachms?

According to the view put forward in the present monograph, the answer to these questions is as short as it is simple. *The later "medallion" types of Kimôn and those of Evænetos were not reproduced on tetradrachms, because by the date at which they were struck, or at least very shortly after their first appearance, the coinage of tetradrachms at Syracuse had altogether ceased.*

It is agreed on all hands that the "medallions" of Evænetos and the later dekadrachm types of Kimôn belong to the Dionysian Period. But these coins present a more advanced style than the signed tetradrachms of Syracuse, and show no traces of transitional epigraphy. They belong to a time when the new letter-forms had finally taken root.

How comes it then, it may fairly be asked of those who bring down the tetradrachms to the same period, that both the style and epigraphy are earlier?

On the other hand, the composition of all large hoards of coins deposited in Sicily about this epoch goes far to explain the break which at this time occurs in the tetradrachm issues of Syracuse. From these finds, and the recent discovery at Santa Maria di Licodia is no exception to the rule, it appears that the silver currency of the Sicilian cities was at this time supplied more and more by *imported Pegasi* of Corinth and her Adriatic colonies. In the recent West Sicilian hoard described under Appendix A, the deposit of which seems to have taken place about 400 B.C., the early didrachms of Leukas were numerously represented. In the great Naxos hoard, buried in all probability about 410 B.C.,[12] these *Pegasi* already occurred in considerable abundance. Add to these a copious supply of Athenian tetradrachms of early style, and, later, the abundant Siculo-Punic coinage, and it will be seen that, without drawing on native Hellenic sources, there was no dearth of silver currency at this time in Sicily. At Syracuse itself the use of the imported silver staters of the mother-city and the sister colonies was quite consistent with local self-respect, and the issue of the splendid *pentékontalitra* of Kimôn and Evænetos might be regarded as a sufficient assertion of the superiority of the city " of great cities" itself.

On the other hand, it is extremely probable that the apparently abrupt cessation of the tetradrachm issues at Syracuse shortly after the commencement of the Dionysian dictatorship, was due to some financial *coup* of that tyrant. Of the expedients to which Dionysios resorted for filling his own coffers we have more than one example. On one occasion, having levied a forced loan of all the available silver in the citizens' possession, he countermarked the coins in such a way as to double their legal value, and repaid his debts in these newly stamped coins, every drachm of silver thus standing for two.[13] Aristotle, to whom this account

---

[12] See Appendix B.

[13] Aristotle, *Oeconomica* II. xx. " Δανεισάμενός τε παρὰ τῶν πολιτῶν χρήματα ἐπ' ἀποδόσει, ὡς ἀπῄτουν αὐτόν, ἐκέλευσεν ἀναφέρειν ὅσον ἔχει τις ἀργύριον πρὸς αὐτόν · εἰ δὲ μὴ, θάνατον ἔταξε τὸ ἐπιτίμιον. Ἀνενεχθέντος δὲ τοῦ ἀργυρίου, ἐπικόψας χαρακτῆρα, ἐξέδωκε τὴν δραχμὴν δύο δυναμένην δραχμὰς τό τε ὀφειλόμενον πρότερον ἀνήνεγκαν πρὸς αὐτόν." This account is supposed by Salinas (see Appendix A, p. 167) and Garrucci (*Monete dell' Italia ant.*, p. 182) to refer to the Rhêgians whom, according

is due, records another and still more outrageous fiscal
operation carried out by Dionysios at Syracuse, which has
moreover a special reference to tetradrachms. Having
levied a forced loan for the construction and equipment of
his fleet, he repaid it by forcing on his creditors tin coins
of the nominal value of four drachmæ, but which in reality
were only worth one.[14] The scarcity of silver[15] is expressly
alleged as the reason for this procedure of Dionysios.
Otherwise he might simply have repeated his former
operation. It is possible, as has been suggested by M.
Six,[16] that the tin thus utilised was acquired from the
loot of Motya.

Of these tin, or possibly debased silver tetradrachms,
which may, perhaps, be compared with the *potin* coinage
of Lesbos, no example is known to exist.[17] They may

---

to the preceding paragraph, Dionysios had sold as slaves, after
robbing them of everything that they possessed. But, if this
was the case, how could he borrow of them? And, if he did
borrow of them, is it likely that he repaid even half his debt?
The πολῖται referred to were certainly his *own* citizens—the
Syracusans.

[14] Aristot., *Oekon.* ii. 20, and *Pollux* ix. 79. (Cf. Boeckh,
Staatshaushaltung der Athener, i. 690; Holm, *Geschichte Siciliens
im Alterthum*, ii. 145, 445.)

[15] Οὐκ εὐπορῶν ἀργυρίου.

[16] *Num. Chron.*, 1875, p. 29.

[17] M. Six (*Num. Chron.*, 1875, p. 28 *seqq.*) supposes that
bronze pieces are referred to, and identifies them with the large
bronze coins of Syracuse with the head of Pallas, weighing
about 8 Attic drachms (see *infra*, p. 159). He suggests that
these coins may have contained 1 drachm of tin and 7 of copper,
and that Dionysios passed them off as containing 4 drachms of
tin and 4 of copper. He assumes that 4 drachms of tin would
be the equivalent of a copper litra weighing 50 drachms. The
value of the coin actually struck, with only 1 drachm of tin in
place of 4, was, however, about 20 copper drachms, so that
30 copper drachms would be gained on each. The theory is

either have been called in on some subsequent occasion by
the Syracusan Mint officers, or have been melted down for
what good metal they contained. It would probably be
too charitable a view to regard them as having been
intended as tokens gradually redeemable by the Treasury,
such as were undoubtedly the iron pieces (*Sidáreoi*) of
Byzantium, struck for inland circulation.

Yet a certain amount of analogy may be detected between
the two cases. The Byzantines were reduced to an iron
currency among themselves because their silver was required
to purchase corn of the Pontic merchants. The Syracusan
Treasury was drained of its specie owing to the constant
demands of Dionysios for the payment of his foreign mercenaries. It is obvious that, as in the parallel case, however
much Dionysios' own subjects might be put off with baser
metal, the mercenaries required their pay in sterling coin.
The dekadrachms were hardly coined in sufficient numbers
to suffice by themselves for this purpose, and it seems
probable that—in addition to the imported "*Pegasi*"—the
Siculo-Punic and Carthaginian tetradrachms, the types of
which so closely approach those of the Syracusan
"medallions," to a great extent supplied Dionysios' re-
quirements, especially in dealing with the Gauls, Iberians,
and other strange troops in his service. It is even
possible that some of the uninscribed coins of this class,

---

ingenious, but it does not seem to meet all the circumstances
of the case. The operation effected on this occasion by Dionysios
was only an aggravated form of what he had done on the
former occasion. He had levied his former loan in silver, and
he repaid it in coins that at least simulated silver tetradrachms.
These bronze pieces, however, with the dolphins and stellar
device, have no visible relation to the silver issues of Syracuse,
though they represent in a changed form traditional devices of
the earlier bronze coinage.

executed in a specially fine style, were actually struck by his direction.

The fact that Dionysios was responsible for a tetra-drachm coinage in base metal, suggests at least a possible explanation for the cessation of the silver tetradrachm issues shortly after his accession to power. It would even appear that during the last years of his reign the "medallions" themselves may have ceased any longer to be coined. The first issue of Evænetos' silver *pentékonta-litra* has been approximately referred to the year 406, and assuming that the later activity of this artist continued for another two decades, he may have engraved his last "medallion" dies about 385 B.C. From the cracked and oxidized character of some of these at the time that the "medallions" themselves were still being struck, it is pro-bable, as has already been suggested, that the dies them-selves continued to be used at a time when the engraver himself had ceased to work. But, even allowing for this prolonged use of these celebrated dies, it is impossible to suppose that they could have been serviceable for any length of time, and it is difficult to believe that the "medallions" were still issued later than at most 360 B.C.

Was the silver coinage of Syracuse, then, altogether in abeyance? It is possible that for a few years this may have been the case, and that the Syracusans were reduced, for a while, at least, to draw on their earlier currency, and on the "Pegasi" or ten-litra staters, as they were known in Sicily, of the Corinthian mother-city and the sister colonies. But if so, there are, I venture to think, good reasons for believing that the want of an independent mintage was soon supplied by the issue by Syracuse herself, and with her own civic inscription, of "Pegasi" copied from the Corinthian models.

With regard to the date of the first issue of these
Syracusan Pegasi, various opinions have been put forward.
Raoul Rochette,[18] the Duc de Luynes,[19] and more recently,
Mr. Head,[20] have connected the first appearance of this
Corinthian type upon the Syracusan dies with the expedition of Timoleón (344 B.C.). M. Six,[21] on the other hand,
would refer the earliest issue of coins of this type to the
reign of Dionysios I., and considers that they were struck
with a view to the commercial interests of Syracuse on the
East Adriatic coast, on which Dionysios had planted his
colonial foundations of Issa and Lissos.

But the style of these staters is hardly early enough for
the reign of Dionysios the Elder, while on the other hand
it still seems to be separated by too long an interval from
that of the Agathokleian "Pegasi" to be well brought down
as late as Timoleón's time. The occurrence on some
examples of the early orthography ϚΥΡΑΚΟϚΙΟΝ also
points to a comparatively early date. On the whole then,
it seems preferable to adopt the view put forward by
Padre Romano,[22] and to connect the first appearance of
these coins with Diôn's successful expedition of 357 B.C.
Diôn on his exile had transported the moveable part
of his large patrimony to Corinth,[23] and that city became
both the financial and military base of the expedition that
he subsequently led to Sicily from Zakynthos.[24] In this

---

[18] *Annali dell' Inst. di Arch.*, 1829, pp. 334—5.
[19] *Rev. Numismatique*, 1843, p. 8.
[20] *Coins of Syracuse*, pp. 28—29 ; but in the *B. M. Cat.*,
" Corinth," Introduction, p. l., Mr. Head prefers " to leave the
question of the exact date an open one."
[21] *Num. Chron.*, 1875, pp. 27—28.
[22] *Sopra alcune monete scoverte in Sicilia* (Paris, 1862), p. 23.
[23] Plutarch, *In Dione.*
[24] Diodôros, lib. xvi., c. 6.

connexion the contemporary appearance of a Leontine Pegasos in precisely the same style as the earliest Syracusan, and with the civic legend in the archaic form ΛEONTINON, has a special significance. Leontini, in fact, specially distinguished itself by the aid that it had afforded to Dión's cause. This city had seized the opportunity of his descent on Syracuse to throw off the Dionysian yoke;[25] with Syracusan aid it had successfully repulsed the attempt of Dionysios II's general, Philistos, to recover it for his master, and shortly afterwards, on Dión's temporary withdrawal from Syracuse, it had afforded him a welcome rallying point for his mercenaries.[26] It is highly probable that the appearance of these two sister types of Corinthian origin at Leontini and Syracuse is to be referred to this moment of close alliance and revived autonomy.

At the time of Timoleón's expedition, on the other hand, the part played by Leontini was very different. It was at this time the rallying point of the tyrant instead of the deliverer. It was not indeed till 340 B.C. that Timoleón was able to make himself master of the city and drive out Hiketas. Leontini, unlike nearly all the other Sicilian cities, so far from being restored to independence was incorporated in the Syracusan territory and its inhabitants transplanted to Syracuse.[27] These alliance pieces with the Corinthian type cannot certainly be referred to Timoleón's time.

It seems to me that the archaic form taken by the inscription on these parallel pieces, which conflicts with

---

[25] Diod., lib. xvi., c. 16.
[26] Diod., lib. xvi., c. 17.
[27] Diod., lib. xvi., 82; Plutarch, *Timoleón*, 32. Cf. E. H. Bunbury, *Smith's Dict. of Geogr.*, *s.v.* Leontini.

their decidedly later style, finds its most rational explanation in the gap which, as has been shown, existed to the
Syracusan coinage. Had the Syracusan tetradrachms been
struck during the Dionysian period, the later epigraphy,
such as we find it on the "medallions," would by this time
have taken such firm root at Syracuse, that to revive the
earlier O for Ω in the civic legend must have savoured
of pedantry. But such, as we have seen, was not the case.
The native silver coins of this denomination on which the
Syracusans, and for that matter the Sikeliote Greeks in
general, still drew, so far as their needs were not supplied
by the imported currency or by the great *pentēkontalitra*,

Figs. 11 and 12.—"Pegasi" struck by Leontini and Syracuse in alliance,
357 B.C.

had none of them been issued in the immediately preceding
period. The date of their issue went back *per saltum* over
a generation to a time when the newer letter forms had
not yet finally taken root. Among the Syracusan and
Sicilian tetradrachms such as we find them in hoards of
coins dating from the Dionysian period the coins with the
older form of epigraphy are still in the majority. Hence,
from the point of view of the die-sinker and moneyer, who
simply reproduced the most frequent form of the civic
inscription as he found it on the current coins of Syracuse
still in use in this day, nothing was more natural than
to write it in the older form ϹΥΡΑΚΟϹΙΟΝ.

To the same period as these early "Pegasi" must

unquestionably be referred the large bronze pieces of Syracuse, presenting a head of Pallas in an olive-wreathed helmet on their obverse and the two dolphins and "webbed" star on the reverse,[28] as well as the smaller bronze pieces, in which the head of the same Goddess is associated with a sea-horse. That these coins belong to an earlier date than Timoleôn's time may be further inferred from the extremely fine copy of Evænetos' head of Persephonê with which the larger of the two coins[29] was over-struck at Kentoripa (Pl. VI. fig. 4),[30] and which from the character of the art displayed it is difficult to bring down later than to the middle of the Fourth Century B.C.

---

[28] Head, *Coins of Syracuse*, Pl. VII., 1, and p. 30. It is there referred to Timoleôn's time.

[29] *Op. cit.*, Pl. VII., 2, and p. 30.

[30] The coin from which the prototype on Pl. VI., fig. 4, was taken, was obtained by me at Centorbi itself. The helmet of the original Pallas is clearly visible on it. I am unable to agree with Mr. Head (*Coins of Syracuse*, p. 36) that the Korê as she appears on these coins bears the stamp of the Agathok-leian Period.

ON A HOARD OF COINS RECENTLY DISCOVERED IN WESTERN SICILY.

THE remarkable hoard recently found in Western Sicily (according to my own information at a place called Contessa), and described by Professor Salinas in the *Notizie degli Scavi* for 1888,[1] has such an important bearing on our present subject as to demand some special notice, the more so as nothing more than brief references to it have appeared in any numismatic publication.

The hoard itself may be summarised as follows :—

Athens.

1. Tetradrachms of fine archaic style 2

Leukas.

2. Several *Pegasi* belonging to the earliest class of Leukadian *Pegasi* . . . . . *x*

Rhégion—Tetradrachms.

3. *Obv.*—Seated Dêmos and insc. ꓱONIꓛƎꓶ.
   Rev.—Lion's scalp 1

4. *Obv.*—In later style with head of Apollo to r., resembling those signed by Kratisippos; in front PHΓINON; behind two leaves and berry.
   Rev.—Do. 1

---

[1] *Ripostiglio Siciliano di Monete Antiche di Argento.* Thanks to the courtesy of Prof. Salinas, I had an opportunity of inspecting these coins when at Palermo.

Akragas.

5. Archaic tetradrachm, worn 1
6. Tetradrachm of fine style, with *obv.* two eagles devouring hare.

    Rev.—Skylla beneath crab ; Insc., **ΑΚΡΑΓΑΝΤΙ-NON**. (Fine condition) 1
                         — 2

Kamarina.—Tetradrachm.

7. *Obv.*—Bearded head of Hêraklês. Insc., **ꟼΑΜΑꓘ**.

    Rev.—Victorious quadriga galloping. (Style of Eumenês.) Swan below. (Somewhat worn) 1

Katanê.—Tetradrachm.

8. *Obv.*—Head of Apollo. Transitional style. **ΚΑΤΑ-NAION.**

    Rev.—Slow quadriga. Two vars. (One in good condition, one rather worn) 2

9. *Obv.*—Head, less archaic, **ΚΑΤΑΝΑΙΟΝ.**

    Rev.—Victory above slow quadriga . . . 1
                         — 3

Eryx.—Tetradrachms.

10. *Obv.*—Seated Aphrodite holding dove, and Erôs ; **ΕΡΥΚΙΝΟΝ.**

    Rev.—Victorious quadriga (fast). In fresh condition 4

Gela.

11. Transitional tetradrachms. Insc., **ϹΕΛΑϞ** and **ϞΑΛƎϽ** 8

Later tetradrachm—

12. *Obv.*—Insc. **ϹΕΛΑϞ·Ꞌ**

    Rev.—Fast quadriga crowned by Nikê. The head of the charioteer turned back 1

(All 9 tetradrachms of Gela were "anterior to the period of developed art," and somewhat worn.)
                         — 9

Himera.—Tetradrachm.

13. *Obv.*—Nymph sacrificing at altar, and Seilênos bathing at fountain. (Fine style.)

    Rev.—IMEPAION; slow quadriga crowned by Nikê. (In fine condition) 1

Leontini.—Tetradrachms.

14. *Obv.*—Head of Apollo.

    Rev.—Lion's head and four grains of corn. Insc., ΛΕΟΝΤΙΝΟΝ, ΝΟΝΙΤΝΟΞΛ, and ΛΕΟΝΤΙΝΟΝ. (Worn) . . . 3

Messana.—Tetradrachms.

15. *Obv.*—Hare to r., spray below **MESS NOINA** with seated driver.

    Rev.—Biga of mules walking; leaf below . . 1

16. Similar, without spray on *obv.*. 1

17. Do. insc. **ME ⋜ ⋞ANOIN** 2

18. Do. *obv.* insc. **ME ⋜ ⋞ANION**; beneath hare a dolphin.

    Rev.—Driver standing, Nikê above; in ex. leaf and berry 3

19. Do. Nikê stands on reins 2

20. Do. Nikê reaches fillet to mules; in ex. two dolphins 2

21. Do. fly beneath hare.

    Rev.—Leaf and berry in ex. 1

22. Do. ear of corn beneath hare.

    Rev.—Female charioteer; above **ME ⋜ ⋞ANA**; in ex. two fishes 1

23. Do. *cicala* beneath hare **NOINA ⋝ ⋝ ƎM**.

    Rev.—Same 1

24. Do. dolphin beneath hare (N)**OINA ⋝ ⋝ ƎM**.

    Rev.—Same. Insc. **A . . . ⋝ ƎM** round . . 1

25. Do. eagle seizing serpent beneath hare. Above to r. in small letters ME Ƨ ƧANIΩN.

    Rev.—Biga of mules walking. Niké holds out a *caduceus* in r. hand, and with l. offers the charioteer a wreath. In ex. dolphin. On exergual line the signature KIMΩN is clearly visible.[2] (Brilliant condition) . . . 1

Motya.—Tetradrachms.

26. *Obv.*—Eagle with closed wings; r. above insc. 𐤀𐤕𐤅𐤌 (*Ha Motua*).

    Rev.—Crab, fish beneath in concave field . . . 1

27. Do., but without fish on reverse 1

[These coins are copied from those of Akragas; but the fish on the reverse shows the influence of a somewhat later Akragantine coin than that from which the obverse is taken. It is found coupled with the crab on an Akragantine tetradrachm, presenting on the obverse an eagle tearing a hare (*B. M. Cat., Agrigentum*, No. 59), of the finest period of art. This fact has an important bearing on the chronology of these Motyan types].

28. *Obv.*—Female head in net to r., copied from the Arethusa of Kimôn's later " medallion," type II.; insc. 𐤀𐤕𐤅𐤌

    Rev.—Crab 1

29. *Obv.*—Female head in net to l. (inferior copy of preceding), but with three dolphins round.

    Rev.—Crab 3

        (On these coins see pp. 67, 68). — 6

Segesta.—Tetradrachm.

30. *Obv.*—Naked male figure to r. before term: two dogs at his feet.

    Rev.—Persephoné in galloping quadriga crowned by Niké. In ex. *cicala* and insc. ƧELE(Ƨ) ΤΑΙΙΑ 1

---

[2] This fact is not noted in Signor Salinas' description. I ascertained it by a personal inspection of the coin.

Selinûs.—Tetradrachm.

31. *Obv.*—Naked River-God sacrificing before altar and ·
holding branch. Before altar a cock ; in field
celery-leaf, ⋝ΕΛΙΝΟΝΤΙΟΝ.

   Rev.—Apollo and Artemis in **slow quadriga, wreath
above** ; below, fish 1

Syracuse.—Tetradrachms.

Archaic types with legend ⋝ΥΡΑΚΟ⋝ΙΟ𝐍.

32. *Obv.*—Female head bound with diadem. 4 vars   . 4

33. *Obv.*—Female head with hair hanging down. Same
inscr., four dolphins bound 1

34. *Obv.*—Female head in less archaic style, **hair bound
with diadem.** Same inscr. &c. .   .   . 1

35. *Obv.*—Similar, but hippocamp in ex. of *rev.* .   . 1

36. *Obv.*—Female head in *sakkos*. Same inscr. .   . 1

37. *Obv.*—Female head with hair bound **by a broad
band. ⋝ΥΡΑΚΟ⋝ΙΟΝ**.   .   . 1

38. *Obv.*—Female head with spiral earring and hair bound
tutulus fashion. Same inscr. &c.   .   . 2

39. *Obv.*—Do. **with hair** bound **up on top of head, same**
legend. Galloping quadriga. In ex. **hippo-
camp** 1

40. *Obv.*—Do. diademed to l. **⋝ΥΡΑΚΟ⋝ΙΟΝ.** Same
rev. but two fishes in ex. 1

41. *Obv.*—**Do.** with spiral earring to l. ; hair bound with
sphendonê, the front adorned with **star** ; be-
neath, signature **ΕΥΜΕΝΟΥ**.

   Rev.—Galloping quadriga drawn by nude winged
figure. In ex. Skylla and signature ΕΥΘ . 1

42. *Obv.*—Do. hair flying up. Type of Eukleidas.

   Rev.—Galloping quadriga, &c.; in **ex.** dolphin. . 3

43. *Obv.*—Do. with *opisthosphendoné* . Φ . . on *ampyx*
(Phrygillos.) Inscr. ⋝ΥΡΑΚΟ⋝ΙΟΝ.

Rev.—Niké above fast quadriga, holding wreath and *aplustre*. In ex. ear of barley and signature EYAPXIΔA. (Figured in *Num. Chron.*, 1890, p. 301) 1

44. *Obv.*—Do. in *opisthosphendonê* bound in front with a fillet (*fiocco*). She wears a circular earring with various pendants ("ha un orecchino a cerchio e vari pendenti"), and a necklace with a small globe.

Rev.—Female driver, in galloping quadriga, crowned above by Niké. In ex. ear of corn . . 1

45. *Obv.*—Do. with spiral earring and *opisthosphendonê* to l.

Rev.—Galloping quadriga, &c. In ex. ear of corn . 1

46. *Obv.*—Do. in starred *opisthosphendonê* with earring of three drops, to l. Inscr.[⋞YPAKO]⋞IΩN.

Rev.—Galloping quadriga, &c. In ex. ear of corn . 2

47. Dekadrachm of Kimôn. Head of Arethusa in the net in high relief. Type II. (Slightly worn.) . 1

48. Dekadrachm of Evænetos. Head of Persephonê, &c. No symbol. The lower part of the coin where the signature EYAINE probably stood is wanting.

Rev.—Quadriga, &c. Horses in fairly high action . 1
(Brilliant condition.)

49. Do. Beneath chin Δ. Under lowermost dolphin EYAINE.

Rev.—As preceding. AΘΛΛ visible beneath panoply in ex. (Brilliant condition.) . . . 2

————
26

Siculo-Punic.

50. *Obv.*—Forepart of bridled horse r., crowned by Victory ; grain of barley in front.

Rev.—Date palm and inscr. 𐤌𐤓𐤀𐤄𐤋𐤕𐤒. Kart-Chadasat 2

51. *Obv.*—Same. Traces of inscr. beneath horse.

Rev.—Same, but no inscr. 1

52. *Obv.*—Same inscr. *Kart-Chadasat* beneath horse.
    Rev.—Same inscr. 𐤌𐤇𐤍𐤕 (*Machanat.*) . . 2

53. *Obv.*—Forepart of horse without bridle r., Victory
    above placing wreath on its head; grain of
    barley in front.
    Rev.—Same, inscr. *Kart-Chadasat* 1

54. *Obv.*—Same, but to l.
    Rev.—Same, inscr. *Kart-Chadasat* . . . 1

55. *Obv.*—Same; two pedestalled cups beneath horse
    interrupting the inscr. *Kart Chadasat.*
    Rev.—Same, inscr. *Machanat* 2

56. *Obv.*—Same.
    Rev.—Same, inscr. *Kart-Chadasat* . . . 1

57. *Obv.*—Free horse galloping r., crowned above by Vic-
    tory.
    Rev.—Date palm 4

58. *Obv.*—Female head with hair flying up and *opistho-
    sphendonê*, copied from Syracusan type of
    Eukleidas (cf. No. 42) (Salinas reads K . . . .
    on the ampyx, and 𐤑𐤉𐤑 = *Ziz*, in front of
    head.)
    Rev.—Galloping quadriga. In ex. mæander . . 1

59. *Obv.*—Female head in net, copied from Kimôn's early
    "medallion," type II.
    Rev.—Galloping quadriga, &c. In ex. hippocamp, and
    inscr. 𐤑𐤉𐤑 2

60. *Obv.*—Female head in net, copied from Kimôn's later
    "medallion," type II.
    Rev.—Same 1

61. *Obv.*—Female head to l., with diadem, on front of
    which is a *Swastika.*
    Rev.—Same 5

62. *Obv.*—Same, higher relief.
    Rev.—Same 1
                                        ——
                                        24

(The Siculo-Punic coins were all in a fine state of preservation.)

ANALYSIS OF HOARD.

Athens	2	Brought forward	. .	24
Leukas	1	Himera	. . .	1
(Several others not described)		Leontini	. . .	3
Rhêgion	2	Messana	. . .	15
Akragas	2	Motya	. . .	6
Kamarina	1	Segesta	. . .	1
Katanê	3	Selinûs	. . .	1
Gela	9	Syracuse	. .	26
Eryx	4	Siculo-Punic	. .	24
	24			101

Professor Salinas,[3] noting that the later of the two tetradrachms of Rhêgion found, though in brilliant condition, only weighs 15·22 grammes instead of the normal weight of somewhat over 17 grammes, attempts to explain this deficiency by a financial expedient recorded of Dionysios.

Aristotle,[4] after relating the shameful behaviour of Dionysios to the Rhêgians, whom he first plundered and then despite his promises sold into slavery, proceeds in the following paragraph to relate how he cheated " the citizens " by levying a forced loan on them and repaying it in money stamped in such a way that every drachm had a fictitious value attached to it of two drachms. This passage Garrucci,[5] Sambon,[6] and after them Salinas, apply to the Rhêgians, but as shown above [7] the πολῖται referred to are Dionysios' own citizens, the Syracusans. The Rhêgians had been already treated in a much more drastic fashion. The transaction mentioned by Aristotle could not indeed in any case be taken to explain the comparatively slight deficiency of weight in the present tetradrachm. Dionysios' fraud was of a much more wholesale character, and brought him in 100 per cent. profit, not merely 12 per cent., as in this instance. The words of Aristotle, moreover, do not at all imply that Dionysios went through the expensive and tedious process of issuing a new

---

[3] Op. cit., pp. 10, 11.
[4] Oeconomica, II. xx.
[5] Le Monete dell'Italia Antica, p. 162.
[6] Recherches sur les Anciennes Monnaies de l'Italie Méridionale, pp. 215, 221.
[7] See p. 153.

coinage, but rather that he countermarked[8] in a certain way the existing coins. The tetradrachm itself, which still displays the earlier orthography PHΓINON, is by no means the latest of the Rhêgian series,[9] and should on grounds of style be referred to a date many years earlier than Dionysios' capture of the city.

The solitary argument adduced for bringing down the date of the deposit of this hoard to after 387 B.C., the date of the capture of Rhêgion, will not bear the test of examination. It is, indeed, in the highest degree improbable that any tetradrachms at all were struck at Rhêgion so late as the above date.

However this light-weight Rhêgian coin is to be explained, it is evident from a general survey of the contents of the hoard that it was withdrawn from circulation at a considerably earlier date.

Amongst 66 Sicilian Greek coins found in this deposit, including specimens from Akragas, Kamarina, Katanê, Gela, Eryx, Himera, Leontini, Messana, Segesta, Selinûs, and Syracuse, Ω appeared only on a single coin (out of 15) of Messana, and on two tetradrachms and four dekadrachms of Syracuse. The coin of Messana on which it appears is the remarkable piece bearing Kimôn's signature on the exergual line of the reverse, and the design of the biga of mules here executed by this artist seems to me to be distinctly earlier in style than that which appears on his earliest dekadrachms. This coin is therefore in all probability not later than about 413 B.C. The three "medallions" of Evænetos found belong to his earlier works of this class.

Among the coins found of Akragas, Gela, Kamarina, Katanê, Himera, and Selinûs, in no case were the latest types of these cities represented.

Making every allowance for the comparative rarity of the later issues belonging to the troubled period of Sicilian history that begins with the Carthaginian invasion of 409, as also for the fact that this hoard was found in the Western and Punic or Elymian part of the Island, it seems impossible, in view of this conspicuous deficiency in the latest types of so many cities, to bring down the date of this deposit much later, say, than the overthrow of Akragas and Gela in 406—5 B.C.

Among the latest coins found in the hoard are, as might be expected, the brilliantly preserved Siculo-Punic series, with the

---

[8] "ἐπικόψας χαρακτῆρα."

[9] Cf., for instance, the type published by Dr. Imhoof-Blumer, *Monnaies Grecques*, Pl. A, 9.

legends *Kart-Chadasat* and *Machanat*, representing the first
issues of the Carthaginian "camp money," struck about 406—
405 B.C. To these must be added the equally well-preserved
coins of Motya with Phœnician legends, and those inscribed
Ziz, which must in all probability be referred to the Panormitis.

The imitations of both the first and second types of Kimôn's
dekadrachms which appear on these latter, show that the
deposit must have taken place some few years at least after the
earlier issues of the Syracusan "medallions" by this artist.
The brilliant condition of all the Siculo-Punic coins discovered
forbids us, however, to believe that any of them had been long
in circulation at the time when this hoard was deposited.

On the other hand, the noteworthy absence of that numerous
class of Siculo-Punic coins presenting copies of the head of
Korê on the "medallions" of Evænetos, makes it improbable
that the hoard was deposited after 393 B.C., about which date
the Carthaginian coins rendering artistic homage to the Persephonê of Syracuse were in all probability first issued.

Taking one indication with another, we may regard 400 B.C.
as approximately the latest date at which this West Sicilian
hoard could have been withdrawn from circulation.

ON THE DATE OF THE GREAT NAXOS DEPOSIT.

IT has been assumed by Padre Giuseppe Romano (*Sopra alcune Monete scoverte in Sicilia*, Paris, 1862), and by Professor Salinas (*Notizie degli Scavi*, 1888, p. 302), that the great hoard of over two thousand Sicilian Greek coins discovered on the site of Naxos (Schisò) in 1853, was deposited at the time of Dionysios' destruction of that city (*c.* 403 B.C.). Were this view correct, the entire absence of Syracusan dekadrachms in this deposit might be urged as an argument for bringing down their first emission at least to the last three years of the Fifth Century.

Miserable, however, as are our sources for the contents of this great hoard, they at least afford conclusive evidence that it was withdrawn from circulation several years before 403.

The first account of this discovery was given in a short communication to the Roman Institute by Padre Pogwisch (*Bull. dell' Inst.*, 1853, p. 154), which was afterwards supplemented (*Bull. dell. Inst.*, 1853, pp. 155—7) by a somewhat fuller, though quite summary, report by Don Giuseppe Cacopardi, who, however, groups another find recently made at Reggio with the Naxos hoard.

In 1854 Riccio (*Bull. dell' Inst.*, 1854, p. xxxix. *seqq.*) basing his account on various consignments of recently discovered coins that had passed through his hands at Naples, gave what professed to be an account of three finds made in 1852—3 in the neighbourhood of Reggio, Messina, and on the site of Naxos. Riccio, however, once more jumbles the separate finds into one account, and even this strange hotch-potch is not, as far as can be judged, very scrupulously described—witness his splendidly vague citation of Castelli's plates. To cap this discreditable performance, moreover, he throws in with the rest yet another find that had been recently made at Noto, consisting chiefly of coins of Hierôn II. and Philistis (Cf. Romano, *op. cit.*, p. 51). Finally, Cavedoni (*Bull. dell' Inst.*, 1855, viii.) gravely supplies a commentary on Riccio's jumble without detecting anything remarkable in the mixture of the finest Fifth Century types with those of a date two centuries later, or even observing the absence of intermediate issues.

To arrive at a basis for obtaining some knowledge of the latest types in the Naxos hoard, we have the following considerations to guide us :—

1. The Reggio hoard is described by Cacopardi as consisting exclusively of "bigas" (*sic*). It follows, therefore, that the coins described as exhibiting "quadrigas," *i.e.* displaying the four horses clearly distinguishable from their high action, belong to one of the other finds.
2. The Noto coins consisting of Hierôns, *Philistideia*, Ptolemies, &c., may be easily eliminated.
3. In the case of Riccio's jumble the Messina hoard still remains an unknown quantity.[1] It is obvious, however, that when (the Third Century coins of the Noto find having been eliminated) the types of any city do not come down to a certain date, it shows that the examples of those types represented in the Naxos find do not come down *beyond* this term, though they do not necessarily reach down to it.

The crucial test of the date of the Naxos deposit is certainly supplied by the coins belonging to Naxos itself, which were specially numerous. Of those described by Cacopardi, there were many of "*seconda grandezza*," representing Dionysos in "Etruscan style," in other words, the earliest of the Naxian types struck before *c.* B.C. 480. The next class, with the head of Dionysos in Transitional style, was also numerously represented. Of those of the finest style, upon which the head of Dionysos is seen surrounded with an ornamental diadem, Cacopardi only noticed a single example. Out of 170 Naxian coins seen by Riccio there were about 20 of the earliest class with the pointed beard, but the bulk were of the Transitional style. Only 6 were of the fine period. From both accounts it appears that not only were the tetradrachms of the fine style very sparsely represented, but that the later Naxian types, on which the ivy-crowned head of the young Dionysos and the laureate head of Apollo make their appearance, were entirely absent.

---

[1] Cacopardi seems to regard the coins found near Messina as of very late date, bordering, in fact, on the Norman period. Riccio, however, leads us to infer that a find of early Greek coins had been made at Messina.

The bulk of the Katanæan coins again were of the ordinary, *i.e.* Transitional style. There were two or three examples of later coins engraved by Evænetos in his early "manner" (the head of Amenanos and of Apollo with Delphic fillet). Two facing heads occur, but full-facing heads had appeared at Selinûs and Syracuse before 409. The works of Hèrakleidas and Choiriôn that characterize the last period of the Katanæan coinage, were apparently conspicuous by their absence.

The quick quadrigas of Himera struck by 409 B.C. were unrepresented. The only coin of Eryx was a small Transitional piece, and no tetradrachm was found. The coins of Segesta seem to have been mostly of earlier types, and no tetradrachms of this city occurred.

Not a single gold piece was found ; but the gold coinage had been introduced at Akragas, Gela, and Syracuse, about the time of the Athenian siege, or earlier.

On all these grounds it seems to me that it would be highly unsafe to bring down the date of the Naxos deposit later than 410 B.C. The account of the Syracusan coins discovered in the hoard is vague and unsatisfactory—Riccio referring to whole pages of Castelli at a time! It appears certain, however, that one specimen of Eukleidas' tetradrachm with the three-quarter head of Pallas was discovered : an interesting indication of the comparatively early date of this type. As a matter of fact, this design by Eukleidas is coupled at times with a reverse design, probably from the hand of Evarchidas, and greatly resembling those in which Nikê holds an aplustre, in commemoration of the sea victory over the Athenians in 413 B.C.

SOME NEW ARTISTS' SIGNATURES ON SICILIAN COINS.

I.—AN EARLIER KIMÔN AT HIMERA.

DURING a recent journey to Sicily I obtained a tetra-drachm of Himera, which may be said to open a new chapter in the history of artists' signatures on Greek coins. The tetradrachm in question (Pl. X. 1*a*) is of the kind presenting on the obverse a quadriga, crowned by a flying Nikê, in which the horses are seen in a somewhat higher action than the better-known early transitional type[1] where they seem to be merely walking. In the present instance the nearer forelegs are raised somewhat higher from the ground, and convey the impression that the horses are breaking into a trot. In the exergue, moreover, the retrograde inscription ᴍƎᴘΑΙΟᴎ is divided by the old canting badge of Himera (quasi ἡμέρα) "the bird of day." This obverse type differs from any in the British Museum; it is found, however, on a coin in the Museo Nazionale at Naples, though in this case the obverse design has been falsified by means of tooling. The head of the cock in the exergue below has been thus transformed into a horned and bearded head of Pan, in blundered imitation of the human-faced

---

[1] Head, *Historia Numorum*, Fig. 78, p. 126.

monster with horns and wings whose forepart appears on contemporary litras of this city.[2]

The reverse of the coin presents a variation from the usual Transitional design. The Nymph Himera is seen clad in a sleeved tunic and *peplos*, with her left hand raised and her right hand extending a *patera* to sacrifice over a garlanded altar, with gabled top, that stands to her right. To the left is a small Seilen taking a douche bath beneath the lion-headed fountain which represents the neighbouring hot springs—the Thermæ Himerenses that still gush forth in the modern town of *Termini*. Above the left hand of the Nymph, as if tossed into the air, is a single barley-corn, indicative, perhaps, of the character of the offering. Though in its general scheme answering to the usual design on the Himeræan tetradrachms of the Transitional class, there are visible in the present example certain differences both in style and details. The folds of the *peplos* are executed with surpassing delicacy and fineness, and cover more of the bosom than is usual in later examples. The Nymph's back hair is not, as on the later Himeræan tetradrachms of this class, contained in a *sphendoné*, but is caught up behind by a diadem, from above which it protrudes in a bunch (*krobylos*) as on early coins of Syracuse, Segesta, and elsewhere. This arrangement is identical with that of the same Nymph's hair as

---

[2] This coin is described in the *Catalogo del Museo Nazionale di Napoli: Medagliere*, 4429. The author of the Catalogue, not observing the falsification, has described the cock in the exergue as having a satyr's head. The head of the charioteer and of the flying Niké above have also been tooled on this example past recognition. Happily the reverse of the coin has remained untouched, and is given in Pl. X. fig. 1*b* as supplying a better representation of the design than my own specimen, though the part of the altar presenting the inscription is blurred.

it appears on the early didrachm of Himera with the legend **IATO𝗡**.

The most interesting feature of the coin, however, remains to be described. A minute examination of the reverse revealed to me the fact that the upper part of the altar, immediately above the cross-moulding beneath the pediment, bore upon it an inscription. Examining this with a lens I read it **KIMON**.[3]

Fig. 13.   (4 diams.)

Although I subsequently examined the coin repeatedly and in different lights, both with magnifying glasses of various powers and with my naked eyes, and obeyed in a literal manner the precept :—

"Nocturnâ versate manu, versate diurnâ,"

I could only return to my original reading. Conscious, however, of the great discrepancy of date between the known pieces with the signature of Kimôn and the present example, and not wishing to trust my unaided judgment in the matter, I submitted the coin to a succession of practised numismatists, without, however, giving them any clue to the name that I had myself made out. Amongst those who examined the piece may be mentioned Messrs. R. S. Poole, B. V. Head, H. A. Grueber, and W. Wroth, of the British Museum ; Professor Percy Gardner,

---

[3] The outline of the **M** and **O** is imperfect and not so clear as that of the other letters. The **K I** and **N** are unmistakable.

of Oxford, and Professor J. H. Middleton, of the Fitzwilliam Museum, Cambridge, and Dr. John Evans. All these authorities not only agreed as to the fact that there was an inscription on the altar, but in each case, after minute examination, came to the independent conclusion that the letters upon it spelt the name of Kimôn. The present signature, extraordinarily minute as it is, must, therefore, be regarded as as well ascertained as that on any other Sicilian coin.

The importance of this fact will be understood when it is remembered that the tetradrachm on which it appears is of a distinctly earlier date than any known example of a coin presenting an artist's signature, either in Sicily itself, or in any other part of the Greek world.

The date of the present type may be approximately fixed on several grounds. Its early " transitional" style itself affords sufficient evidence that the piece before us was struck at a date considerably anterior to the later class of tetradrachms exhibiting more advanced versions of the same design. Yet, in 409 B.C., when the Carthaginians took Himera and razed it to the ground, this later class had itself already yielded to a still more developed type, presenting on the obverse a quadriga with horses in high action. On the other hand a *terminus a quo* is supplied by the domination of Thêrôn, of Akragas, and his son, Thrasydæos, from B.C. 482 to c. B.C. 470. It is to this period that the Himeræan drachms and didrachms, exhibiting upon their reverse the Akragantine crab, must unquestionably be referred, and it was, in all probability, during the years that immediately succeeded the recovery of Himeræan independence, about 470 B.C., that the coins representing the Nymph Himera sacrificing were first struck. The earliest coin of this new series seems to be

the didrachm with the mysterious legend IATON on the
reverse, and from the fact that the tetradrachm with which
we are concerned attributes to the Nymph the same archaic
type of head-dress that characterizes the didrachms with
the above legend, it is evident that its issue must approximately belong to the same period. Upon the later tetradrachms this archaic top-knot is abandoned, and we may,
therefore, infer that the present coin belongs to the earliest
class of tetradrachms struck by this city.

It is probable, indeed, that the type in which the Nymph
is seen throwing up a wheel in place of the barley-corn,
and which displays the figure of the Seilen in profile,[4] is
slightly anterior in date to the present example; but with
this exception the coin before us, presenting the signature
of Kimôn, must be regarded as the earliest of the Himeræan issues of this denomination, and it would be certainly
unsafe to bring down its approximate date lower than
450 B.C.

The improvement perceptible, alike in the design and
execution of the present tetradrachm, as compared with the
other, and, as the identity of the Nymph's coiffure shows,
nearly contemporary type, supplies convincing evidence
that the engraver who has here attached his name to the
reverse was an artist of no mean capacity. The bathing
Seilen, with his head bent back and looking round towards
the spectator, his wrist turned in and pressed against his
side as if in the act of rubbing it, and his whole expression
and attitude instinct with animal enjoyment, is itself a
masterpiece for the numismatic period in which it makes
its appearance. It strikingly recalls the pictorial method
of treating similar subjects, as seen, for instance, on the

---

[4] B. M. Cat. No. 32.

remarkable polychrome amphora found at Vulci,[5] in which four naked women are represented taking a douche-bath from as many spouts in the shape of the open jaws of lions and boars; or, again, on a black-figure vase in the Leyden Museum,[6] where youths and men are exhibited disporting themselves after the same manner. Equally admirable is the rendering upon this coin of the diaphanous folds of the Nymph's Ionic mantle, which for lightness and delicacy of touch is unique in the Himeræan series.

It is evident that the Kimôn who signs on these coins cannot be the artist of that name who attaches his signature to the fine tetradrachms and pentêkontalitra of Syracuse struck during the last two decades of the Fifth Century B.C. But in view of the well-known Greek practice of repeating personal names in alternate generations and the prevalence of hereditary succession in artistic industries, of which we have a striking numismatic example in the case of the celebrated group of Syracusan die-sinkers, the probability that the earlier Kimôn was the grandfather of the later becomes considerable. The number of artistic engravers whose signatures appear on the Sicilian dies is still so limited, that such a coincidence of names must in any case be regarded as a highly suggestive phenomenon. On the other hand the interval—exceeding one generation—

[5] Gerhard, *Etruskische und Kampanische Vasenbilder d. k. Museums zu Berlin*, Taf. 30 ; Lenormant et De Witte, *Élite des Monuments céramographiques*, iv. 18 ; Baumeister, *Denkmäler des klassischen Alterthums*, i. p. 243. Rayet and Collignon (*Histoire de la Céramique grecque*, pp. 106-7) remark of this amphora, "peut-être ce joli vase sort-il d'un des ateliers des colonies chalcidiennes de la Campanie; voir même d'une des fabriques de quelque cité dorienne de la Sicile ou de la grande Grèce."
[6] Roulez, *Choix des Vases peints du Musée de Leyde*, Pl. XIX. 1, p. 79 ; Daremberg et Saglio, s.v. *Balneum* (i. p. 649).

between the activity of the two homonymous engravers
fully accords with such a relationship.

It is to be observed that at Syracuse itself, Kimôn's name
does not, except in the solitary instance of a hêmidrachm
signed **IM** on the obverse,[7] appear associated with that
of any other engraver on the same coin. Both the obverse
and reverse designs of the coins signed by him are from
his own hand.[8] In this respect he stands quite aloof
from the well-known group of engravers to whom two-
thirds of the signed coins of Syracuse belong, Eumenês,
Eukleidas, and Evænetos,[9] the two latter of whom occasionally attach their signatures to pieces the other side of
which is engraved by the earlier and less advanced
Eumenês, to whom they probably stood in a filial relation.[10] Kimôn himself appears at Syracuse, as the independent contemporary and rival of the two younger
artists, and there is no evidence in his case of any pre-
existing connexion with Syracuse.

On the other hand it is a noteworthy fact that outside
Syracuse, we find the evidence of this later Kimôn's
activity on the coins of the Chalkidian city of Messana,[11]
and there are some reasons for believing that he also
worked for the Rhêgian mint. His signature reappears
at Metapontion, and there is circumstantial evidence of
his connexion with the Chalkidian cities of the Campanian
coast.[12]

---

[7] B. M. Cat. *Sicily*, p. 181, No. 233.
[8] See p. 77.
[9] To these may be added the artist who signs Euth, on a
reverse coupled by an obverse by Eumenês, and Phrygillos who
is in the same way associated with Euth . . . , and Evarchidas.
[10] See Weil, *Die Künstlerinschriften der Sicilischen Münzen*,
p. 52.
[11] See below, p. 186—188.
[12] See p. 75 *seqq.*

If we may believe that this later Kimôn was himself a scion of the great Chalkidian foundation of the North Sicilian Coast, it would go far to explain the apparent geographical range within which his works were executed.[13]

II.—MAI . . . AT HIMERA.

There exists a remarkable tetradrachm type of Himera distinguished from all other varieties by its advanced style, and obviously dating from the period which immediately preceded the destruction of the city by the Carthaginians, which has long, with good reason, been suspected of having originally contained an artist's signature.[14] This is the piece [15] upon which there appears above the quad-

---

[13] A further argument might be adduced for connecting this Kimôn with the North Sicilian Coast were it possible to accept Professor Salinas' suggestion (*Notizie degli Scavi*, 1888, p. 310; and cf. Tav. xviii. 33) that a Siculo-Punic tetradrachm (probably struck at Panormos) with a Phœnician inscription in the field, bears his signature. The letters on the *ampyx* of the sphendonê-band, however, on which Professor Salinas relies, are by no means clear, and the head itself is, to my mind, a Siculo-Punic copy of a fine Syracusan type by the engraver Eukleidas. Professor Salinas' observation that the attitude of the charioteer on the reverse recalls that on a reverse accompanying Kimôn's celebrated design of the facing Arethusa (*op. cit.* Taf. iii. 10a) is certainly just, but the scheme of the horses is in this case different and hardly Kimônian.

[14] Cf. for instance, Weil, *Künstlerinschriften*, &c., p. 28.

[15] B. M. Cat. No. 48, where it is described as follows : "Nymph facing, head l., wearing sleeved chiton and peplos, the ends of which fall over r. arm ; she holds in r. hand patera over altar with square horns ; behind her a Seilen, facing, bending sideways to receive on his l. shoulder jet of water issuing from a lion's head fountain.—Quadriga r., driven by charioteer wearing long chiton who holds reins in both hands ; horses in high action ; above, Nikê l. holding wreath and tablet. In ex. sea-horse, l."

riga, on the obverse side, a small figure of Nikê bearing
aloft a suspended *pinakion* or tablet, in a manner precisely
similar to that exhibiting the signature of Evænetos on a
well-known tetradrachm of Syracuse.[16] On the Himeræan
example in the British Museum, the tablet held by Nikê
is unfortunately quite smooth and without a trace of let-
tering; on a specimen, however, in the Paris Cabinet des
Médailles, (Pl. X. fig. 2), I have now succeeded in detecting the actual inscription, of which an enlarged copy is
here given:

Fig. 14.   (4 diams.)

The first stroke of the **M** is somewhat indistinct, but
the remaining part of the inscription is clear.   It can
only be read **MAI**,[17] in which we are at liberty to seek the
name of the engraver, Mæôn [18] perhaps, or Mæthiôn.[19]

The tetradrachm in the Paris Cabinet is further epi-
graphically important from the inscription traceable on
the exergual space beneath the Nymph, a part of the coin
which is wanting in the British Museum specimen.   It
reads **Ͱ I**, which by analogy with the inscription **IMEPA**
in the field beside the female figure on the earlier tetradrachm of this city having on its reverse the figure of
Pelops with his name attached,[20] may be taken as giving

----

[16] B. M. Cat. No. 188; *Künstlerinschriften*, &c. T. ii. 1.

[17] M. Babelon, to whose courtesy is due the impression of
this piece figured on Pl. X. 2, agrees in this reading.

[18] C.I.G. 2855.

[19] C.I.G. 4437.

[20] Friedländer, *Berliner Blätter*, &c., i. 137; v. 4; Imhoof-
Blumer, *Monnaies Grecques*, Pl. B, 3.

the first syllable of the name of the Nymph Himera.[21] This appearance of the form Ͱ is unique on the coinage of the Sicilian cities. It is noteworthy, however, that at Himera itself a great variety is observable in the initial letter of the name of the city and its eponymic Nymph. In the early period the aspirate is consistently given in the form H ; on the tetradrachms, however, struck after *c.* 467, it disappears, though recurring still on drachms and litras. On Transitional copper coins the inscription **KIMAPA** is found.[22] Finally, on an obol exhibiting on the obverse side a head, as it seems, of Kronos, and on the other a Corinthian helmet, the civic inscription occurs as **ⒷIME**.[23] The present initial Ͱ represents a letter-form peculiar to the Tarentine and Hêrakleian mint, and must

---

[21] It can hardly be a new version of the inscription **IATOⲚ** which occurs in the exergual space of the still earlier didrachms, since this enigmatic inscription is not found on the later Himeræan issues.

[22] B. M. Cat. *Sicily*, p. 81, No. 50, and p. 82, No. 51. These coins are hêmilitra. It may be suggested that the form Kimara should be brought into relation with the he-goat ($\chi i\mu\alpha\rho\sigma$) which appears on the obverse side, and that the adoption of this design on the Himeræan coin as well as that (B. M. Cat. *Sicily*, p. 80, Nos. 41-44) representing the forepart of a winged monster with the horn of a goat, a man's head, a lion's paw, and the head of a lion resting against the shoulder, should be regarded as due to a play on the word *Chimæra*, just as the cock on other coins seems to stand in relation to the form **HIMEPA** *quasi* $\eta\mu\epsilon\rho\alpha$. The early established connexion between the Chimæra and volcanic forces (cf. Fischer, *Bellerophon*, Leipzig, 1851, p. 90 *seqq.*) would give an especial appropriateness to its appearance on the coins of a city famed for its thermal springs. The Lykian Volcano, Chimæra, which served in antiquity as the "local habitation" of the monster, received its name from the probably Semitic Solymi. Fischer (*loc. cit.* p. 93) compares the Hebrew חמר = to roar; to rise as with leaven (specially applied to bitumen or boiling pitch, cf. Gesenius, *s. v.*).

[23] B. M. Cat. *Sicily*, p. 81, No. 46.

itself be regarded as a late form of *Vau*.[24] The appearance of these various equivalents, H, ⊟ K and Ͱ, for the
initial sound of the name Himera seems to indicate
that the original sound was of a complex character,
imperfectly reproduced by any one letter of the Greek
alphabet.

The coin itself is otherwise of great interest owing to
the advanced character of the design on both obverse and
reverse, and the chronological standpoint that it affords us.
The sacrificing nymph and the bathing Seilen are both
free from archaism, and the high and even sensational
action of the quadriga is a striking phenomenon for the
date at which this coin was struck, and which cannot
by any possibility be later than 409 B.C., in which year
Himera itself was utterly destroyed by the Carthaginians.

The overthrow of this city was indeed more complete
than that of any other Sicilian town that at this period
fell into Carthaginian hands, owing to the fact that they
had here the memories of a past disaster,—the greatest
that ever befell them in the island,—to wipe out. It was
beneath the walls of this city that, two generations earlier,
the Carthaginian General Hamilkar and his mighty host
had been slain or captured by Thêrôn and Gelôn, and the
grandson of the fallen commander, Hannibal, the son of
Giskôn, to whose lot it had fallen to lead the successful
onslaught of 409, expiated the former slaughter and
the *manes* of his grandfather by the solemn sacrifice of
three thousand captive warriors and by razing the city

---

[24] Kirchhoff, *Studien zur Geschichte des griechischen Alphabets*
(1887) (p. 146). As a form of Vau in its numeral application
= 6, Ͱ also served to indicate a drachm (= 6 obols). In this
signification it is frequent in Attic inscriptions, but it cannot be
taken as mark of value in the case of our tetradrachm.

to the ground.[25] When, not long afterwards, Hermokratês recovered the site of Himera, it was such a heap
of ruins that he was constrained to encamp outside the
town.[26] The destruction of Himera followed almost immediately on that of Selinûs,[27] and its exceptionally
thorough-going character, of which we have the historic
record, precludes us from supposing that it ever was
in a position to renew its once brilliant coinage. The
remnant of its citizens who survived never seem to have
attempted to restore their fallen city or to reoccupy its
site, but preferred to settle in the new town of Therma,
which the Carthaginians had founded about the hot baths
some few miles distant from Himera itself. Here they
revived the civic issue under the name of the Thermitæ.[28]

The necessity of assigning a date, not later than 409
B.C., to the remarkable piece signed MAI is, as already
pointed out, of further importance in its bearing upon the
chronology of the Syracusan tetradrachm by Evænetos
which has so obviously influenced its design.[29] When it

---

[25] Diodôros, Lib. xiii c. 62:—"Ὁ δὲ 'Αννίβας τὰ μὲν ἱερά
συλήσας καὶ τοὺς καταφυγόντας ἱκέτας ἀποσπάσας ἐνέπρησε καὶ
τὴν πόλιν εἰς ἔδαφος κατέσκαψεν, οἰκισθεῖσαν ἔτη διακόσια
τεσσαράκοντα."

[26] Diod. Lib. xiii. c. 75. Ἑρμοκράτης δὲ . . . . παραγενόμενος
πρὸς τὴν Ἰμέραν κατεστρατοπέδευσεν ἐν τοῖς προαστείοις τῆς
ἀνατετραμμένης πόλεως.

[27] Grote includes the destruction of both cities within the
limits of 409 B.C.

[28] Diod. xiii. c. 79, and cf. Cicero, Verr. II. c. 35. The new
city was founded by the Carthaginians in 407 B.C. previous to
the fresh invasion of Hamilkar and Hamilkôn; it was colonized
by Carthaginian citizens and voluntary settlers from other
"Libyan Cities." Therma (or Thermæ) could not have become
a Greek city till the time of Dionysios' expedition in 396 B.C.

[29] See p. 55. I observe that the striking connexion with the
work of Evænetos has also been recognised by Weil (op. cit. p.
14). "Wie die Nike zeigt auch die Ausführung des Gespannes

is remembered that the action of the horses on the present
coin is decidedly higher and more advanced than on the
tetradrachm by the Syracusan artist from which the Victory and tablet are here borrowed, it becomes evident that
the prototype from Evænetos' hands must have been struck
some years at least before the latest possible date assignable to the Himeræan coin. On the other hand the
agitated scheme of the quadriga on the present coin need
not surprise us. Chariot groups in which the horses are
depicted rearing and plunging in a similar manner, with
their heads violently raised or turned round towards each
other—a certain dualism being perceptible throughout—
appear already on some of the later black-figured vases
and become frequent on those of the succeeding red-
figure style dating from the middle of the Fifth Century
B.C.[30] For a numismatic parallel, contemporary with
the Himeræan design, we have only to turn to some of the
latest hêmidrachms of Selinûs struck in, or shortly before,
409 B.C. It therefore appears, that already before this
approximate date, sensationalism of design had in this
respect reached its acme on the Sicilian dies.[31]

---

besonderheiten die sich nur bei Euainetos wiederfiden, mit
dessen Tetradrachmen Taf. II. n. 1, III. n. 6. hier auffallende
Verwandschaft bemerkbar wird."

[30] Compare, for example, Lenormant and De Witte, *Élite des
Monuments céramographiques*. T. I. Pl. xi, III. Pl. xv, II. cix,
cx. The last example shows a considerable conformity with
the design on the Himeræan tetradrachm by MAI . . .

[31] Professor Gardner, indeed, in his "Sicilian Studies"
(*Num. Chron.* 1876, p. 24) makes the climax arrive later. "At
Selinus, destroyed in 409, the horses still move steadily and
soberly. At Himera, which fell four years later, they are more
restive and their heads are turned in various directions, but
their feet still keep time. At Catane, which struck coins for but
two years longer, they are still more in disorder, the rein of one
is flying loose, and there appears close to them a meta which they

III.—THE LATER KIMÔN AT MESSANA.

In the hoard recently discovered at Santa Maria di Licodia, in Sicily, there occurred a tetradrachm of Messana of a hitherto unpublished type and presenting features of the greatest interest.[32] Upon this coin (Pl. X. 3a), which has the further peculiarity of exhibiting on its reverse an *apéné* or biga of mules in high action, the head of a Nymph is seen in the space beneath the part of the obverse occupied on some varieties of the Messanian coins by the youthful head of Pan. Around this head is visible an inscription in minute letters, which, with the aid of another example of the same piece in the *Cabinet de France* (Pl. X. 3b), I have been able to decipher. The inscription informs us, what might seem probable on other grounds, that the Nymph represented is Pelôrias, the personification of the promontory in the neighbour-hood of Messana which forms the N.E. extremity of Sicily and is now known as *Capo del Faro*.

Below the neck of the Nymph again, on my example,

---

seem scarce likely to round in safety. At Syracuse, which alone survived, we find broken chariot wheels, overthrown metas and other picturesque accessories." But—1. As noticed above, the hémidrachms of Selinus already show very high action. 2. The destruction of Himera followed that of Selinus after an interval at most of a few months (*v. supra.*). 3. The incident of the trailing rein occurs already in the Syracusan design by Evænetos from which the Himeræan artist MAI drew, and Syracusan tetradrachms with quadriga types in high action, representing much the same stage of artistic evolution as that of the same Himeræan piece, are associated with comparatively early heads of Arethusa by the engraver Phrygillos. 4. The broken wheel occurs on a type by Evænetos, more or less contemporary with that presenting the signed tablet and associated with a comparatively early obverse head by Eukleidas.

[32] See p. 18, No. 23.

are visible further traces of minute letters. The inscription is, unfortunately, by no means clear, but the two final
letters are, apparently . . . ΩN, and the signature must
in all probability be referred to the artist, Kimôn.

The following is the full description of this remarkable
piece :—

> *Obv.*—Biga of galloping mules driven by apparently female
> charioteer, crowned by flying Nikê. In ex.,
> barley-spike.

> *Rev.*—ΜΕ𐤮𐤮ΑΝΙΟΝ in f. above hare, running r.
> Beneath, Nymph's head, her back-hair contained
> in a *sphendonê.* In the field, in front of her face,
> the inscription ΓΕΛΩΡΙΑ𐤮, and below the
> neck . . . . ΩN (?). To the right of the head
> is a cockle-shell and to the left a corn-spike.

It has been already suggested by Messrs. R. S. Poole and
Percy Gardner[33] that another tetradrachm of Messana contains traces of Kimôn's signature on the exergual line
beneath the biga. The coin in question is the fine type
on which an eagle devouring a serpent is seen beneath
the hare, while Nikê on the other side holds a caduceus
as well as a wreath; and from a comparison of several
specimens of the same type in other collections, I am able
wholly to corroborate the suggestion of the authors of the
Sicilian volume of the British Museum Catalogue. On a
specimen belonging to a great hoard recently discovered in
Western Sicily,[34] the last four letters of Kimôn's name are
clearly decipherable, and the whole or greater part of the
signature ΚΙΜΩΝ is visible on other coins of this type
which I have been able to examine in the Naples and Paris

---

[33] B. M. Cat. *Sicily,* p. 105, No. 56.

[34] Published, though without the signature, in the *Notizie degli
Scavi,* 1888, p. 218 and Tav. xvii. 4.

Cabinets, the collection of Dr. Imhoof-Blumer, and elsewhere.   It is noteworthy that both this and the newly-discovered coin belong to the transitional epigraphic period
when the Ω and upright N was just coming into use.   In
the former case we find the Ω already adopted, but both N
and N—the N in the civic inscription, the later form in the
signature, KIMΩN.   On the coin presenting the Nymph's
head the O is retained in the civic inscription but is replaced by the later form in the name ΓΕΛΩΡΙΑϹ, and
the final syllable of the signature.   The same phenomenon
recurs in the case of the tetradrachm signed by Sôsiôn
at Syracuse.[35]   Both from this epigraphic peculiarity and
from the general style of the engraving, as well as the
comparatively early representation of the bigas, we may
infer that these Messanian works of Kimôn are earlier than
his Syracusan dies.   A considerable resemblance is, however, perceptible between the head of Pelôrias on the
Messanian coin, and that of Arethusa upon Kimôn's earliest dekadrachms,[36] the correspondence in the formation
of the eye being specially remarkable.

The head of Pelôrias is known on Messanian drachms
and bronze coins, her hair in some cases being wreathed
with corn, but otherwise unconfined.   On a bronze piece
she is seen with a *sphendonê* and earring, while beneath
her neck is a dolphin.   In the present instance the
twofold aspect of Pelôrias, both as a fertile inland range

---

[35] The civic inscription is ϹYPAKOϹΙΟN, the signature on
the ampyx is ϹΩϹΙΩN, showing both the later form Ω and N.
See Weil, *op. cit.* p. 7, Taf. 2, 4 ; Von Sallet, *Zeitschr. f. Num.*
T. II. No. I. (Berlin) ; B. M. Cat. *Sicily*, p. 167, No. 154. The
signature is hardly traceable, however, on this specimen, and
the suggested reading Ϲ[ΩϹ]ΩN seems to be corrected by
the Berlin example.

[36] See B. M. Cat. *Sicily*, p. 175, No. 200.

and its seaward continuation, a mere sandy spit, is indicated by the double attributes, the ear of corn and the cockle-shell, the latter symbol being placed in front of the Nymph's face, just as the *syrinx* in front of the young head of Pan on a parallel Messanian type. The cockle in the present connexion has a special significance, since the sandy point of Pelôros contains between the beach and the hills two large sheets of water called the Round and Long Lakes, which produce the best cockles in Sicily. These are still reared with great care, being planted in rows by the natives,[37] and their celebrity in ancient times is more than once referred to by Athenæus.[38]

IV.—EVARCHIDAS AT SYRACUSE.

The name of the artist Evarchidas has been recently added to the roll of Syracusan engravers by Professor Salinas.[39] With the aid of a coin belonging to an important hoard recently brought to light in Western Sicily, the learned Director of the Museum of Palermo has successfully demonstrated that a reverse type, attributed by Raoul Rochette and others to Eukleidas, presents

---

[37] Smyth, *Sicily*, p. 106.
[38] Athen. i. p. 4, c; iii. p. 92, f. Cf. E. H. Bunbury in Smith's *Dict. of Antiquities*, *s.v.* "Pelorus."
[39] *Notizie degli Scavi*, 1888, p. 307, *seqq.* and Tav. xvii. fig. 25. Raoul Rochette (*Lettre à M. le Duc de Luynes sur les graveurs des Monnaies grecques*, p. 29), following an error of Castelli's, had attributed the coin to an artist of the name of "Nouklidas," for which (*Lettre à M. Schorn*, &c., p. 92) he afterwards substituted "Eukleidas," in which emendation he was followed by Streber (*Die Syrakusanischen Stempelschneider Phrygillos Sosion und Eumelos*), Weil (*Dei Künstlerinschriften der sicilischen Münzen*, p. 18) and Von Sallet (*Die Künstlerinschriften auf griechischen Münzen*, p. 21).

in reality the legend EYAPXIΔA. While recently in
Palermo I had an opportunity of verifying the correctness
of this reading, and by the kindness of Professor Salinas
I am able to include in Pl. X. (fig. 7) a phototype of
the piece in question. The head on the obverse side is
by Phrygillos, and bears traces of the inscription ΦΡΥ
on the front band of the *sphendonê*, while EYAPXIΔA
is clearly legible beneath the exergual line on the
reverse.[40]

Fig. 15.   (4 diams.)

On a very similar type[41] the same inscription is seen
above the exergual line immediately below the horses'
forefeet.

Professor Salinas has called attention to two specialities in the above designs of Evarchidas—the fact that
Persephonê, who here drives the chariot, is represented
almost full facing, and that Nikê above holds a small
aplustre as well as the wreath. In this naval trophy
he detects a distinct allusion to the sea victory of 413,
won by the Syracusans over the Athenians in the Great

---

[40] Salinas (*loc. cit.*) cites another specimen of this type in the
Luynes Collection.

[41] Three examples exist of this coin—one is in the collection
of Baron Pennisi at Acireale, and is published by Salinas, *loc. cit.*
p. 306, and the two others are in the Cabinets of Berlin and
Munich. The reverse of the first of these, photographed by
Weil (*Künstlerinschriften*, &c., T. i. fig. 12), was by him
erroneously attributed to Eukleidas; the other, published by
Streber (*Die syracusanischen Stempelschneider Phrygillos*, &c.),
was by that writer also ascribed to Eukleidas.

Harbour of the city, which left the land forces of the invaders at the mercy of the conquerors.[42]

Two other tetradrachm reverses have been referred by Professor Salinas to the same engraver. Both show the same disposition of the horses, Persephonê with the torch, Nikê with the *aplustre* and the corn-spike in the exergue. On one of them, however, from the Fox collection, the Goddess appears with a larger body and more flowing locks. On the other, in the Luynes collection, her head is in profile.

Of this latter type I am now able to cite two more examples. One of these, Pl. X., fig. 6*a*, is from the hoard recently discovered at Santa Maria di Licodia, in Sicily. The head, as usual, is by Phrygillos, traces of his signature, ΦΡΥ, being visible on the *sphendonê* band above the forehead; the reverse shows Persephonê with her *peplos* flying up like a hood behind her head, a feature which strikingly recalls the bas-relief of the victory-crowned quadriga from the Parthenon, now in the Elgin room of the British Museum.[43] Nikê is seen above holding the wreath and *aplustre*, and to the right of the car of corn in the exergue are apparently traces of letters. Another specimen, of the same type and on both sides from the same die as the preceding, exists in the British Museum.[44] The obverse of this coin, as being better preserved than that on the Santa Maria example, is given on Pl. X., fig. 6*b*, for comparison. The inscrip-

---

[42] See above, "Syracusan 'Medallions' and their Engravers," p. 131.

[43] *Ancient Marbles*, &c., ix. 33.

[44] B. M. Cat., *Sicily*, No. 159. The reverse of this coin is not so well preserved as that from the Santa Maria find and the exergue is unfortunately far from clear.

tion reading ⋜ΥΡΑΚΩⲊΙΟΝ, presents us with a curio-
sity of transitional epigraphy ;[45] the *aplustre* on the reverse
is wrongly described as "a palm" in the Catalogue.

Accepting Professor Salinas' suggestion that the occasion of these interesting types, in which Nikê bears aloft
the naval trophy, is to be sought in the destruction of the
Athenian fleet in the Great Harbour of Syracuse, we gain
a new and very satisfactory standpoint for the date of
the peculiar scheme of quadriga with which the dies of
Evarchidas are associated.   At Syracuse itself, a very
similar scheme, in which the front pair of horses is seen
with their heads turned back to back, while the third horse
raises its nostrils above the forehead of the second, accompanies the well-known head of Arethusa by Eukleidas
with the upward streaming hair,[46] as also his facing head
of Pallas.[47]   Similar schemes are also found in connexion
with the obverse type signed **ΙΛΛ**,[48] with another head by
Phrygillos,[49] with Kimôn's tetradrachm head of the side-
facing Arethusa in the net.[50]   At Kamarina the same
scheme characterizes the reverses of tetradrachms signed
by Exakestidas ;[51] at Katanê it is seen on the coins signed
by Evænetos,[52] presenting the fine head of Apollo, which

---

[45] See p. 60.
[46] B. M. Cat., 194—195, Head, *Coins of Syracuse*, Pl. IV. 5.
On this and the other parallel cited, however, the head of the
hindmost horse is not turned back as in Evarchidas' design.
[47] B. M. Cat., 198—199.
[48] B. M. Cat., 214.   Head, *op. cit.*, Pl. V. 3.
[49] B. M. Cat., 158.   On the reverse of this coin Persephonê
is seen holding a torch as on the design of Evarchidas.   The
aplustre, however, is absent.   It is possible that this reverse die
must also be ascribed to Evarchidas.
[50] B. M. Cat., 207.   Head, *op. cit.*, Pl. IV. 8.
[51] B. M. Cat., 264.   Weil, *Künstlerinschriften*, &c., Taf. ii. 7.
[52] Weil, *op. cit.*, Taf. ii. 4 and 4a ; B. M. Cat., 85.

must still be described as executed in his earlier manner.
At Agrigentum it occurs on the beautiful tetradrachm
inscribed ᕀΤΡΑΤΩΝ,[53] and a close parallel is found at
Segesta[54] before 410. These equations are calculated to
cast a new light on the chronology of the Sicilian issues of
this period, and show that sensationalism of design in the
quadriga types, which, as has already been noticed in the
preceding section,[55] reaches its acme at Himera in or shortly
before 409 B.C., was already far advanced as early as 413.

V.—PARME . . . AT SYRACUSE.

A Syracusan tetradrachm in my own collection (Pl.
X. fig. 5), recently found near Taormina (Tauromenion),

Fig. 16.   (4 diams.)

supplies a new variety of the signature of the engraver
Parme . . . . . The coin, though from a different obverse
die, presents the same female head, doubtless of Arethusa,
in the star-spangled *sphendoné* as that on the known coins
by this artist,[56] but in this case the letters ΓΑΡ are visible,

---

[53] B. M. Cat., 58.
[54] B. M. Cat., *Sicily*, p. 184, No. 34.
[55] See p. 13 and note.
[56] B. M. Cat., *Sicily*, p. 178, Nos. 212, 213 ; Head, *Coinage of Syracuse*, Pl. V., 1 ; Weil, *op. cit.*, Taf. iii. 11, and p. 20 ; Raoul Rochette, *op. cit.*, Pl. II., f. 17, and p. 30 ; Von Sallet, *op. cit.*, p. 43.

as above, on the front part of the neck immediately above
the necklace (Fig. 16). It will be recalled that this
method of signature corresponds with that adopted by
Evænetos in his facing head of the young River-God
Hipparis on a didrachm of Kamarina. On the other
hand, the appearance of the letters on the neck in this
example, may in this case be simply due to double striking.
The reverse of this coin, in which the horses of the quadriga are seen with a trailing rein trampling under foot a
broken chariot-wheel, is identical with that of some unsigned coins unquestionably by the same engraver.[57]

VI., VII.—SYRACUSAN HÊMIDRACHMS BY EVÆNETOS, AND BY φ AND EY....

A Syracusan hêmidrachm presenting in the exergue of
its reverse a broken chariot-wheel, has already, from the
character of the design, been attributed by Mr. Head to
Evænetos.[58] Whilst recently at Syracuse I acquired
the following hêmidrachm (Pl. X. fig. 9) containing in
the abbreviated form E what must certainly be regarded
as the signature of this artist.

> *Obv.*—Female head to l., wearing star-spangled *sphen-
> doné*, necklace, and, apparently, spiral earring;
> on either side a dolphin head downwards; below
> [ξY]PAKOξION.

> *Rev.*—Quadriga to r., much resembling that of Evænetos'
> signed tetradrachms (B. M. Cat., 188) but with-
> out the trailing rein, driven by male charioteer,
> crowned by flying Niké. In ex. E between two
> dolphins.

> Wt. 28½ grs.

---

[57] B. M. Cat., *Sicily*, p. 178, No. 212, and p. 179, No. 219
(Head, *op. cit.*, Pl. V. 2).

[58] *Coins of Syracuse*, p. 10, and cf. Pl. III.; B. M. Cat., 164,
155.

This coin, it will be seen, is a variety of that given in
the B. M. Cat., *Sicily*, No. 166.

On another Syracusan hêmidrachm in my own collection
(Pl. X. fig. 8),[59] presenting an obverse head somewhat
similar to the above, but with a different profile and with
flowing locks escaping from above the *sphendoné*, the
letter Φ makes its appearance in the space beneath the
chin. From the general agreement of the female head on
this coin with the types of Phrygillos, it is probable that
the obverse type in question must be referred to that
engraver.

Upon the reverse of this piece a scheme of horses appears presenting, perhaps, the greatest resemblance to the
quadriga on a tetradrachm the obverse type of which is
Kimón's famous facing head of Arethusa. It also occurs
on late hêmidrachms of Selinus. The heads of the two foremost horses are in this scheme turned back to back, while
the second and nearer pair have their heads and necks
partly overlapping. In the exergue is an ear of barley,
and to the left of it the letters EY, the inscription being
apparently continued to the right of the symbol, though
it is here, unfortunately, illegible.

It is to be observed that the ear of barley upon the
Syracusan tetradrachms is usually associated with obverse
heads by Phrygillos, while the reverse types that it accompanies seem to be in nearly all ascertainable cases from the
hand of Evarchidas. It is to this artist, therefore, that the
reverse of our hêmidrachm must be preferably ascribed.

---

[59] The weight of this coin is 31 grs.

VIII.—EXAKESTIDAS AT KAMARINA.

The name of the engraver Exakestidas is already associated with two coin-types of Kamarina. In the one case
his signature in the abbreviated form **EΞAKE** between
two upright strokes on a raised band, is seen written back-
wards beneath the head of the young River-God Hipparis,
on a didrachm of that city displaying upon the reverse
the Nymph Kamarina on her swan, clad in a short-sleeved
tunic.[60] In the other case, that of a tetradrachm, the name
EΞAKEϚTIΔAϚ appears in full on the exergual line
of the reverse representing a victorious quadriga in high
action driven by Pallas. In the exergual space below
are two linked *amphoræ*, the prizes of a chariot race in
Athena's honour, full of her sacred oil, and the obverse of
the coin exhibits a singularly youthful head of Heráklês
coifed in his lion's skin.[61]

A highly interesting tetradrachm of Kamarina (Pl.
X. fig. 4) recently acquired by me in Sicily, has now

[60] Salinas, *Rev. Num.*, 1864, Pl. XV. 6, *Le Monete delle Antiche
Città di Sicilia*, Tav. xviii. 2. Von Sallet, *Künstlerinschriften*,
&c. p. 16. Weil, *Künstlerinschriften*, &c., Taf. ii. 8, and p. 14.
This coin is in Dr. Imhoof-Blumer's collection. On a closely
allied type in the B. M., *Sicily*, p. 37, No. 18, an **A**, and perhaps
a part of **K**, are seen beneath the head of Hipparis, which doubtless belong to the same signature. It is probable that all the
reverse types of the Kamarinæan didrachms in which the Nymph
Kamarina is seen clad in a tunic are by the same engraver. On
the design of the Nymph which accompanies the facing head of
Hipparis by Evænetos the upper part of her body is represented
nude.

[61] First published by Raoul Rochette, *Lettre à M. le Duc de
Luynes sur les Graveurs des Monnaies Grecques*, Paris, 1831, p. 32,
and Pl. II. 18. (Cf. B. M. Cat., *Sicily*, p. 36, No. 14; Weil,
op. cit. Taf. ii. 7, and p. 14. Salinas, *Le Monete*, &c., Tav.
XVII. 16.)

supplied the proof that this beautiful **but somewhat effeminate** head of the young God, of which it has been justly observed **that** but for connecting links between the types and the traces of the incipient whisker it might be taken to portray Omphalê rather than Hêraklês,[62] **is also** from the hand of Exakestidas.

The obverse of this coin, the head of which is identical with that **referred to above, and** which contains the civic legend in **the** same form, **KAMAPINAIO N**, displays in the field in front of Hêraklês' **lips** a diptych, as represented below, upon the two leaves **of** which appears the inscription, **EΞAKEꟻ**.

Fig. 17. (4 diams.)

The reverse type of this coin differs in several respects **from** that which bears **the** name of Exakestidas in full on its exergual line. Great prominence is here given to the figure of Athena, who literally towers above **the** chariot and holds in her **right** hand an abnormally long **goad.** The wheel of the chariot—only one is **visible** on this type—is in greater **perspective. Of the horses, the** first three are abreast, their heads and necks **partially** overlapping, and arranged in a slightly ascending scale, while **the** foremost horse plunges forward, and **rears his head** and neck upwards, so as almost to touch

[62] Gardner, *Sicilian Studies* (*Num. Chron.* 1876) p. 32, and cf. his *Types of Greek Coins*, p. 128.

the foot of the flying Victory above. In the exergual space is a barley-corn, and no signature is visible on this side.

An unsigned tetradrachm of Kamarina exists, which, from its great resemblance to the present piece, must be referred to the same engraver.[63]

In this case, in place of the inscribed tablets, there appears in front of the chin of the youthful Hêraklês an olive spray consisting of a leaf and berry. The civic legend takes the later form, KAMAPINAIΩN. The reverse is the same, and on an example in the Naples Cabinet, and another in the British Museum,[64] it is from the same die.

The inscribed diptych on the obverse field of the newly-discovered tetradrachm by Exakestidas recalls that containing the name of Eukleidas, which occurs in much the same position on a Syracusan piece.[65] The Syracusan tetradrachm type in question represents the earliest work of Eukleidas of which we have any knowledge, and the two reverses with which it is coupled are both signed by Eumenês, and executed in the rude early manner of that artist. Syracusan influence is very marked on the dies of Kamarina, and we have, indeed, the evidence of Evænetos' signature on the most beautiful of the

---

[63] Salinas, *Le Monete*, &c., Tav. xvii., 17 ; B. M. Cat., *Sicily*, p. 36, No. 15. Gardner, *Types of Greek Coins*, Pl. VI. 15 and 17. Head, *Historia Numorum*, p. 122, fig. 69, where, however, it seems to be wrongly implied that the signature EΞAKE ≶ TIΔA≶ is associated with the reverse of this type.

[64] Gardner, *Types of Greek Coins*, Pl. VI. 27.

[65] B. M. Cat., *Sicily*, p. 173, No. 193. Von Sallet, *op. cit.*, p. 22. Raoul Rochette, *op. cit.*, Pl. I. 2. The reverse in these cases signed EYMHNOY. Weil, *Künstlerinschriften*, &c., Taf. iii. The reverse signed EY.

didrachm types of this city to show that a colleaguo of
Eukleidas actually worked for the Kamarinæan mint. The
quadriga types of Kamarina may, perhaps, in all cases, be
traced back to Syracusan prototypes, and the scheme of
the horses on the present piece, though immediately
derived from the groups that appear on two· slightly
earlier tetradrachms[66] exhibiting the bearded head of
Hêraklês, must be regarded as in the second degree an
outgrowth of the arrangement adopted by Evænetos in a
fine early design that accompanies an obverse head signed
by Eukleidas.[67]

These typological considerations, as well as the general
style of the design and engraving, incline us to place the
new work of Exakestidas very late in the Kamarinæan
series. On the other hand the existence of a very similar
type without the signature and with the civic inscription
in a later style of epigraph, characterized by the upright
N and Ω for O, precludes us from bringing down its date
of issue as late as 405 B.C.

---

[66] Salinas, Le Monete, &c., Tav. xvii. 5 and 6.

[67] B. M. Cat., Sicily, p. 173, No. 190. Weil, op. cit., Taf. iii.,
6. This design, in which the signature EYAINETO appears
on the exergual line, is almost literally copied in the Kamarinæan
quadriga given in Salinas, op. cit., Tav. xvii. 5, an overturned
meta being substituted for the broken wheel in the exergue. The
Syracusan reverse by Evænetos (already referred to, p. 12, as the
source of a late Himeræan type), in which Nikê is seen bearing
aloft the inscribed tablet, also stands in a near relation to these
designs. These quadriga types by Evænetos are themselves
developments of an earlier scheme associated with the signature
of the older master, Eumenês.

APPENDIX

A SUPPLEMENTARY specimen from the Santa Maria hoard has now enabled me to detect a new form of Kimôn's signature on the reverse of a fine Syracusan "Medallion" of his second type. The obverse of this coin presents the signature $\frac{KI}{M}$ on the band above the forehead as it appears on Kimôn's earliest deka-drachm type, and in this case, too, there is no trace of letters on the dolphin beneath Arethusa's neck. The reverse, on which the arms and the inscription ΑΘΛΑ below them are well preserved, shows the usual traces of the full form of the name KIMΩN on the upper surface of the exergual line, but over and above this it presents the retrograde and abbreviated signature $\frac{IX}{M}$ in the space between the reins and the haunch of the nearest horse. We have thus, for the first time, a reverse parallel to the reduplication of Kimôn's signature in a full and a shortened form which characterizes the obverse of his later "Medallions." In both instances we may venture to detect, as I have already suggested in the case of the Velian and other Magna Græcian and Sicilian artists,[1] a reference to the double character in which Kimôn was connected with the Syracusan dies.

In the more conspicuous signature, here the letters in the field, he must be held to sign as a responsible mint official. In the almost imperceptible reproduction of his name above the exergual line he unquestionably signs in a purely artistic capacity.

Another example of this interesting piece, and from the same die, exists in the Cabinet des Médailles, and is reproduced as a fine specimen of Kimôn's second style on Plate II., Fig. 1.

---

[1] *Horsemen of Tarentum*, p. 116 *seqq.*

INDEX.

PRINTED BY J. S. VIRTUE AND CO., LIMITED, CITY ROAD, LONDON.

Evmenēs ——— Evth   Late Transitional (Syr.)

Evaenetos (Syr)   Kimòn: First Medallion Type.   Segesta

Parme... (Syr.)   Syracuse

Panormos, imitated from Kimòn, Type I

PLATE I.

KIMÔN'S FIRST MEDALLION TYPE AND ILLUSTRATIVE COINS.

Kimôn, Type II

2

Kimôn, Type II

Kimôn, Gold Stater
as Type II

Kimôn, Tetradrachm
as Type II

4ª

4ᵇ

Kimôn, Gold Staters
(Later)

5

6

Motya : Imitations of Kimôn's Type II

7

Kimôn, 'Medallion' Type III

Panormos, Im. of K. T II

Didrachms of Neapolis

PLATE II.

KIMON'S LATER 'MEDALLIONS' AND ILLUSTRATIVE COINS.

Neapolis

Phistelia

Tetradrachms by Kimôn with Facing Head of Arethusa

Katané (Choirion)   Himera. Æ Motya, Æ   Kamarina, Æ

Motya Didrachm   Motya, Æ   Motya Didrachm

Larissa (Thessaly)   Satrapal Coin of
Cilicia Æ

PLATE III.

KIMÔN'S FACING HEAD OF ARETHUSA. PROTOTYPE AND COPIES.

Evaenetos, Gold
Pentékontalitron

Evaenetos, Gold Staters

5

Gem found near
Catania

6

Tarsos Æ
(Tersikon)

Carthaginian
Gold Pieces

9

Carthaginian
Camp Coin

10

Evaenetos, Earliest
Medallion Type

11

12

Evaenetos (Evaine)

Evaenetos
with Δ on Obv

13ª

13ᵇ

Evaenetos : Latest Medallion with Signature Evainetov

PLATE V.

'Medallion' of Evaenetos

Agathoklēs

Kentoripa Æ

Hiketas N

Opuntian Lokrians

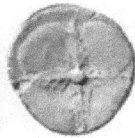

Pheneos

Rhoda

Massalia

Emporiae

Siculo-Punic

Hérakleia
Minoa   Siculo - Punic Æ   Panormos

   5———————5

Carthaginian N

Siculo - Punic Æ

      Katanê

Syracuse

Katanê   Kamarina

COINS IN EVAENETOS EARLIER MANNER.

PLATE VIII.

'MEDALLION' OF KIMON (TYPE I). *ENLARGED TWO DIAMETERS*

PLATE IX.

'MEDALLION' OF EVAENETOS. *ENLARGED TWO DIAMETERS*

Pl. X.

AN
EARLIER
KIMÔN

1 a

AT
HIMERA

1 b

MAI
AT
HIMERA
2

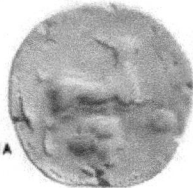

3 a

3 b

THE
LATER
KIMÔN

AT
MESSANA

EXAKESTIDAS
AT

PARME.
AT

4

KAMARINA

5

SYRACUSE

6 a

6 b

PHRYGILLOS AND EVARCHIDAS, SYRACUSE

8

7

9

Φ AND EY... SYRACUSE

PHRYGILLOS AND EVARCHIDAS
SYRACUSE

EVÆNETOS
SYRACUSE

NEW ARTISTS' SIGNATURES ON SICILIAN COINS.

Numismatic and other Archæological Works

BY THE SAME AUTHOR.

THE "HORSEMEN" OF TARENTUM: a Contribution towards the Numismatic History of Great Greece. With 11 Autotype Plates. 8vo, cloth, 12s. 6d.

"This monograph on this particular coinage of Tarentum is one of the most complete and exhaustive of its kind, and moreover illustrates the remarkable advance which has been made of late years in the study of Greek numismatics.

"We need scarcely add that monographs of this description are of the highest importance to archæologists as well as to numismatists. Coins have one special feature above all other objects of antiquity, such as sculpture, terra-cottas, vases, bronzes, and gems, inasmuch as they are capable of being dated often to within a few months of their issue, almost without exception to within a very few years To one important authentic piece of sculpture we have at least five hundred coins which show Greek art in all its phases, from archaism to a condition of perfection, and again downwards in its various stages of degradation. They act, in fact, as guides to the dating of every other class of object, and, as such, archæologists cannot neglect their study.

"The work is well supplied with indices and also with illustrations done by the autotype process, which are of the greatest use in following the learned author's arguments and reasonings."—*The Athenæum*, March 8th, 1890.

ON A LATE CELTIC CEMETERY AT AYLESFORD, KENT.

> PART I.—The Cemetery and its Contents.
>
> ,, II.—The Late Celtic Pottery of the Aylesford Urn-field; its Gaulish Extension and Old Venetian (Illyro-Italic, &c.) Sources.
>
> ,, III.—The Aylesford Bronzes.
>
> ,, IV.—General Conclusions as to the Date and Character of the Aylesford Cemetery. (Contains an investigation of the sources of Ancient British Culture.)

Reprinted from *Archæologia*. With 6 Plates and 19 Woodcuts in the Text. Quarto, 10s. 6d.

ANTIQUARIAN RESEARCHES IN ILLYRICUM.

> PARTS I. & II. Contain Researches into the Roman, &c., Remains of Dalmatia.
>
> PARTS III. & IV.—Explorations of the Roman Sites and Road-lines of the Interior of the Balkan Peninsula: Bosnia, "Old" Serbia, Albania, and N. Macedonia, including Scupi (Usküp), the birthplace of Justinian. (This section contains the first archæological investigation of the Roman Province of Dardania).

With Maps showing the ancient Sites and Road-lines, and Facsimiles of Inscriptions, and other illustrations. Reprinted from *Archæologia*. Quarto, price 18s.

Agent—BERNARD QUARITCH, 15, PICCADILLY, LONDON.

www.ingramcontent.com/pod-product-compliance
Lightning Source LLC
Chambersburg PA
CBHW030358270326
41926CB00009B/1164